"Being A Real Man"

By M. R. Michaels

ISBN #978-0-692-25647-3

Introduction

The achievement of your goal is assured, the moment you commit yourself.

Being a real man is a chronicle of a man's journey where he found himself hitting rock bottom and climbed his way back to the top. It is a tale that describes how God came into his life and drastically changed it.

This text will help you understand why you would want to have a relationship with God and what can happen if you choose not to do so. It will inspire you as well as teach you the basics of Christianity and the advantages of such.

It will encourage you to surround yourself with the right kind of people as well as aid you if you are undecided what is truth or not. It will further you to make the right decision for your life.

Jeremiah 29:11; "For I know the plans I have for you", declares the Lord. "Plans to prosper you and not harm you, plans to give you hope and a future".

Contents

Chapter 1

The Early Years

"You can't know where you're going until you know where you have been."

There were many days when I genuinely believed this quote was written about my life. It is a stepping-stone to understanding where I am now in relation to my walk with the Lord. My childhood was atrocious and my adulthood even worse. For me, spiritual growth took time, experience, and many mistakes. But, ultimately, it was God's love that steered me in the right direction.

I was an athlete for a large portion of my life. In high school, I played football and wrestled and continued my love for sports once I entered the Army, as well. Then, what seemed to be overnight, I found myself at thirty-five years old with my muscles getting softer and my beer gut getting bigger. I didn't even recognize myself. Determined to get back at least a portion of the physique I once took so much pride in. I headed down to the gym at my apartment complex.

As I entered the gym with determination in my eyes, I noticed another gentleman already working out. He looked around my age, my build, and adorned in an Army t-shirt. I wondered if he had faced a similar epiphany as I had. I decided to strike up a conversation since I, too, was an old Army chap. We compared adventures and duties and I found myself genuinely enjoying our discussion.

After exercising, we began to exit the gym and he asked me a question that threw me off guard. "Have you ever thought about Jesus and making Him your Lord and Savior?" He asked as if he already knew the answer. I politely answered, "No". I wondered if I came off as needing spiritual guidance or if it was merely a question. He reached into his gym bag and pulled out a brochure with his church's information on it. He invited me to be a guest. I thanked him as we went our separate ways. I truthfully had no intention of going. But, for the first time, I gave his question some thought. "Hmmm," I thought to myself.

"Accepting Jesus into my life, could my friends and family see me now". While I pondered his question more. I felt embarrassed as I recalled our conversation and how much I swore during it.

What you have to understand is that I criticized God and religion for years. I went to Sunday school as a child but didn't learn much. Nor did I have an understanding of what it meant to go to church and develop a personal relationship with God. The only basics I retained were what society as a whole already knew; Adam and Eve were the first people on Earth, Jesus was the son of God and died on the cross. As well as a reference to Moses, I probably got most of that from the movie The Ten commandments. I didn't know how or why these things pertained to religion and I didn't care either. I didn't know God. That made it easy for me to criticize. It's effortless for people to criticize what they don't know or understand.

I used to think that all people that went to church were pathetic, damaged, and/or had low self-esteem. I

was a jock with a natural ability to do almost anything I
wanted and an inflated ego to go along with it.

I had friends and girlfriends that tried to encourage
me to go to church. However, it was more fun to go to
the bars, get drunk and sleep in, than to get up on
Sunday morning and go to church. What was the
reason? It was pointless in my eyes. I felt that I didn't
need to be lectured every Sunday by hypocrites.

Let me give you another example of what I am talking
about. In 1988, when I was assigned to my new Army
base in Germany, there was a private who I got the
distinct "honor" of meeting. We'll call him Private
Edwards for privacy purposes. He was a character! He
was a self-proclaimed Christian. His behavior, however,
supported my previous beliefs. He had no self- esteem,
he was a religious nut and pretty much an outcast from
everyone within the unit. He had some very peculiar
habits. For instance, he would walk down the halls of
the barracks with one shoulder brushing up against the
wall. Then, he would suddenly make a complete stop,
do a right or left face, cross the hallway, and again walk
down the hall with his other shoulder brushing against

the wall. When he was asked why he walked in such a peculiar way, he replied, "The devil is on my trail and I have to shake him off!"

When Edwards first arrived at our unit he was a specialist, or pay grade E-4, therefore, he was given his own barracks room. He would leave his light on all night. His reasoning was "I'm waiting for my family to come home, so I have to leave the lights on to let them know I'm here." It didn't make sense. Family members were not allowed to live in the barracks. They were rarely allowed to visit.

One night a couple of us went to the post Burger King where we found Edwards sitting in a booth all by himself, yet he had four trays of food with him. He told us he was waiting for his family for dinner. That was a little on the strange side. What I later learned was that he had been stationed in Germany before. He had met a single mother, they dated and eventually got married. From my understanding, he also adopted his wife's two daughters. Another oddity was whenever he attempted to unlock his door to his barracks room; he would go through the motion as if he was blessing the door handle with his key. Kind of like the same motion a Catholic would do when they motion their hand from the forehead to the chest and back and forth left to right. The Father, Son, and Holy Spirit motion.

He would also put the key in and then take it out a couple of times, unsure if he wanted to unlock the door or not. One of the strangest activities he had was that he always carried his Bible with him. His Bible was unlike any other that I have ever seen before or since. His Bible had no cover and was in the shape of a ball. It looked like he shredded it and molded it together into that shape. Kind of like paper mache. It was in such disarray that it was almost impossible to read an entire scripture from it.   If you know anything about the Army, the Bible, unfortunately, is not a part of the uniform unless you're a Chaplain. So, he would place it in the cargo pocket of his BDU uniform.

It probably would have gone unnoticed if it hadn't such an unusual shape. He went overboard when he carried it while wearing his PT uniform. He placed it in his pelvic area inside his underwear. It really stood out.

Not to mention, I'm not sure that would be an appropriate place to put
a Bible. Needless to say, he got a lot of ribbing from almost everyone.

He also had a way of defying orders. He refused to carry a weapon and wouldn't stop carrying his mangled Bible no matter what uniform he had on. He refused to partake in any of the day to day activities or whatever training we had. So, he eventually lost rank. What was sad, was it was a pay grade at a time. You would think he would learn after the first time. Regardless of how much rank he lost, he stuck to his way of life.

Because of the demotions, he was forced to share a barracks room with other privates. He refused to stay in those rooms because the other soldiers had posters of popular artists; mostly women taped to their walls and had beer in their refrigerators. We would often find him sleeping in the day room or on the benches in the shower stalls as a matter of protest using his Bible as a pillow. It was times like this that I felt sorry for him. I wondered what had triggered him to start acting in such peculiar ways.

There was this one night when I was sitting in my room relaxing when all of a sudden, I heard a loud scream. It sounded like someone had been murdered. It was gut-wrenching. I ran out of my room to see what was going on. When I looked down the hall, I saw a couple of soldiers laughing. In the middle of them was Private Edwards flipping out. The soldiers had been walking down the hallway with beer in their hands and asked him if he wanted one. He said "No" but they insisted. He repeated himself sternly. One of the soldiers reached out to hand him one anyway and accidentally touched him with the beer. He went nuts! The soldiers roared with laughter. It was just par for the course with this guy. The soldiers made a game out of Private Edwards' idiosyncrasies. They continued touching him with beer to watch his insane reactions. Once the incident started getting out of control, it took a couple of us Sergeants to break up the incident, though we really didn't want to.

My position with the Army at the time was that of the Unit Armorer. I was in charge of all the units' firearms. It was a very conscientious job. I was accountable for every weapon and its whereabouts. I was also trained on how to repair them at a higher level than the average soldier. Six months or so into it, Edwards, now a private with no stripes on his uniform was assigned to me. I was given instructions by my First Sergeant that he was to have severe restrictions. He wasn't allowed to touch anything, he wasn't allowed to do anything, he was to just sit there all day long and do nothing. Basically, I became his full-time babysitter. He was to follow me EVERYWHERE, especially if I had to leave the arms room. He was to be my shadow during regular duty hours…no questions asked. He became a strain on my life.

I was also given extra responsibilities regarding his basic welfare. One time I was asked by the First Sergeant to force him to
take a shower. Let me tell you, that was no fun task. I was finally able to coerce him to take a shower. It was either that or get a couple of guys to help me physically force him. As he showered, he stood away from the trickle of the water while wearing his underwear. He washed himself by cupping his hands under the spray, splashing himself with whatever he caught. All this time

he refused to use shampoo or soap. He told me that
soap and shampoo were tools of the devil. When he
was done. he refused to use a towel to dry off, he just
put his clothes back on.

I also had to make sure he ate chow and slept in his
barracks room (not in the day room or the showers).
After a while, he was given his own room again. His
mental state made it impossible for him to cohabitate
with others.

I found out that he was originally from Colorado. I
tried to extend an olive branch one evening and invited
him to my room to watch the Nebraska vs. Colorado
football game that was on television. He politely
accepted my invitation. When he arrived at my room, he
was so restless. I had to strongly persuade him just to
sit down and relax. He eventually grabbed a chair and
sat next to my wall locker. He seemed to be doing fine
until he turned around and saw all the postcards of
women in bikinis that were taped to the side of my wall
locker. He caused a huge ruckus and needless to say,
the visit didn't last very long. He left immediately.

Then there was the night we had to pull CQ duty together. CQ means we were in charge of the quarters. We were to watch over the barracks in case of any emergencies, as well as keep peace and order. I felt as if no matter what I did I couldn't escape his insanity and religious lunacy. Everywhere I turned, he was there and causing me headache after headache. You can call me a glutton for punishment but that night we discussed God and the Bible. He was very knowledgeable about the Bible and could recite all sixty-six books in chronological order. I wasn't going to question him considering I wouldn't know if he was right or not, but I was impressed nonetheless.

He continued to tell me about God. Like telling me that God was everywhere. "Oh really?" I chided. I stepped outside and said "Where? I don't see him". "God, is that you?" Oh wait, maybe that's Him, standing behind that tree". I laughed at my own jokes but he didn't find them amusing. He also tried to tell me how wonderful God is and how much he loved me but I wasn't buying it.

That night we managed to get back into more serious conversations. I got to learn about the events that led to his current state of mental illness. It took me by surprise that I enjoyed that time with him. He had been to Germany previously, met a woman with two little girls, and got married.

When they eventually went back to the United States, she divorced him. It's not a rare occurrence in the military but it messed him up. It's called the dreaded PX pass, where women take advantage of a military man to get a free ticket to the United States. She hurt him so badly that he completely went over the edge. My heart went out to him. Maybe he wasn't a bad guy after all. He just wasn't sure how to cope with such a tremendous heartbreak. Being back in Germany so far from her and the kids did not help his situation. He sure did have some strange characteristic traits though. Perhaps he was just a product of his circumstances. Little did I know that my life would end up ironically similar.

Though I enjoyed our conversation that night. Considering our exchanges of ideology was so different. It just re-emphasized my previous beliefs. "That all religious people were weak". I didn't need God. I was rough, tough and bullets could bounce off my chest. I learned later after I became a Christian that those people were not weak. What made them different was they had warm hearts and open arms.

My childhood was horrific. When I say that, I am not trying to belittle others who have also endured major tribulations. We all have our own personal horrors. I'm not looking for sympathy. It's just a matter of fact. I was the oldest child of four with two sisters and a baby brother. Because of what I encountered, no matter what, I felt it was my place to protect my siblings.

My upbringing was one of both physical and verbal abuse. The only true signs of affection ever given towards me came from my grandmother. I couldn't grasp the concept of love aside from that. She was my mother's mom and took me in as much as possible and spoiled me rotten, just like grandmothers are supposed to do. Because of that, I tried to see her as much as possible. She was my rock. She lived about fifteen miles away in the town just north of us. When I was very young and went on outings with my mother, I would pay close attention to what direction we were going. Because I knew if we got on certain roads we had a chance of going by to visit her at either her tailor shop or her home. I also knew it was there that I would receive the love that I required.

I can honestly say during my entire childhood. I never once received a hug or kiss from my parents, nor was I told by them that they loved me. Now my grandmother, on the other hand, told me all the time. When I got the opportunity to spend the weekend with her she would always give me a kiss goodnight and tell me she loved me. I was so touched by this that I usually cried myself to sleep.

To give you an idea of what my childhood was like. I want to start from the beginning. My biological father had a severe drinking problem. It was a daily activity of his to go to the bar after work. There were many nights when he never bothered to even come home from the bars. Not too sure if it was because of his girlfriend or if he just got so drunk he passed out. He had a tendency to wreck his car or drive it into a ditch due to his stupor. When he did manage to show his face, he enjoyed using my mother and me as punching bags. He would hit her more often than me and that was because I always did my best to avoid him; oftentimes pretending to be asleep. I never understood his addictions nor the violence but it was the life I was handed. What could I do?

My mother was no angel by any means but, for some reason, she always provoked my father. I'm not too sure why but it sure seemed intentional at times. I'm certainly not saying she deserved to be hit. No woman does. I just felt at times she goaded him. If only she was strong enough to change her circumstances. Usually, after she and my father had an encounter, she would take out her frustrations on not so much me, but my younger sisters. She hit me one time and if my memory serves me correctly. I just laughed at her, I guess because I was used to the force of my fathers' hits it had no impact.

There were so many evenings when I would pray that he wouldn't come home. I never performed the physical act of praying to God, it was probably more of hopeful thinking. Now that I look back, I can guarantee there were nights that God blessed us with my father's absence. Those nights were much better. When he wasn't around and she behaved herself, you could notice the difference of peace and calmness in the house. You could also see that my siblings were completely different. They played, laughed, and were allowed to be kids for a change. Those were the nights that made me realize what life SHOULD be like. It was so enjoyable that the nights my father did come, I hoped it would be the last time.

I was terrified of my father as a child. Rightfully so, I suppose. But that fright ultimately turned to hatred. I vowed that one day I would get even with him. Not so much for beating on me. I was getting tough because of it, but for hurting my mother and siblings. He didn't necessarily punch on them. Instead, he would torture them by folding their fingers down and squeeze them until they turned white. Sometimes he did it for pure pleasure as he would laugh while hurting them. He was a big man who worked in the construction industry and was very strong. I was impressed with his strength physically yet found him to be weak mentally. I once saw him pound a 16 penny nail needing only two hits.

The first one held the nail in place and the second drove it all the way in. I knew that if I was to ever pay him back I needed to be tough both physically and mentally.

For such a strong man, you figured he would have self-confidence. However, when he was in the company of others besides his family or drinking buddies, he acted shy or even stupid along the lines of illiterate. Sometimes, I thought maybe he was putting on a show so that people wouldn't discover the real him.

When my father beat me, he would justify his actions by saying things like, "I'm going to make a man out of you," or "You need to learn how to be a man in order to protect this family". He would tell me that there was no way a kid my size could hit me as hard as he could. If I learned to take his beatings, then I could take a hit that a kid my size would deliver. Talk about a twisted mindset. He also taught me that if someone was causing problems for me that the solution was to beat them up and they would leave me alone. That is parenting 101 at its finest. I know it may seem crazy but eventually, his philosophy started to sink into me to where I became the quintessential bully.

My father had a reputation for hitting guys while they weren't looking. Realistically, he was a coward despite his tough exterior. When I became old enough to go to the bars. There was one particular bar that I would go to and ended up meeting a couple of guys that knew him. One of them was a close friend of his and had shared with me that he had a tendency to fight dirty. There was this other guy who wasn't so fond of him. Apparently, my father got the best of him on more than one occasion. When it came to fighting dirty, my father would say that there are no rules in fighting. Considering how he was raising me. It made sense.

One night when we were all sitting at the bar this guy who didn't like him ran off at the mouth towards me. My father's friend suggested that he was looking to get his revenge by taking it out on me. I pretty much ignored him. Sizing him up, he was no match for me. Later on, he challenged me to a game of pool. He was pretty intoxicated by then. As you can imagine, the alcohol didn't exactly help his pool game. I won the game and he got so upset that he swung his pool cue at me. Mind you I was on the other side of the table and the cue never came close to hitting me. My patience had worn out and I had enough! I asked him to step outside. We went out to the alley where I beat him senseless. It wasn't hard to do considering his condition. As I was assaulting him, I told him to remember what family he was messing with. That it would be wise for him to take his drunken self-home and not to show his face in that bar again. Wow, was I becoming the junior version of my father?

Let me go back a little bit to my grade school days. When I was in kindergarten, I had a kid that would pick on me a lot. At this time, I hadn't gotten a grasp on my father's "teachings" yet. This kid would break my pencils and crayons, steal from me, and hit me from time to time for no apparent reason. Everything a bully is known for doing, he did. I dealt with this little punk for years. At the end of the fourth grade, we moved to a different part of town and I finally didn't have to deal with him anymore…so I thought. After two years of being free from his antics, his family moved into our neighborhood and I was horrified all over again.

One night, I was on my way home from delivering my newspapers. As I got there, I found this kid in my front yard waiting for me. He wanted to fight me...big surprise! I was extremely scared. I ran quickly in the direction of my house, dodging him, and eventually managed to escape his grasp. To my surprise, my father was home and witnessed the entire incident. He beat me immediately for not fighting.

The next night, that persistent kid was waiting in my yard for me again. I didn't know if my father was home or not so I fought the kid in hopes that his beating would be less severe than my father's. I lost the fight, which came to no surprise. It wasn't a gallant effort but I hoped it would save me from a worse demise. I stumbled inside the house and found my father. He beat me again. This time it was for losing.

He said that he would make a man out of me yet. Almost as if he was prophesying his upcoming departure and it would be my responsibility to take care of the family. Each word he uttered, he would hit me harder. It was that day when I vowed to never lose a fight again. That incident dramatically changed me for a long time. Why wouldn't it? I got beat three times in two days and had done nothing wrong. I felt like I couldn't win.

One evening when I was in the seventh grade, my little brother and I went to a high school football game. My brother ran off with a few of his friends and I headed in another direction with mine. Toward the end of the game, a friend of mine saw a boy our age beating up this kid whom he did not know was related to me. My friend intervened and was able to get the boy away from my brother. After he did, he asked my brother, "Where are your parents?" My brother told him that he came to the game with me. So, my friend brought my brother to me and explained what happened.

Guess who the culprit was? It was the same kid that bullied me most of my life and was the cause of my three beatings in two days. I was so angry that every fear I ever had about fighting was instantly gone. I was consumed with anger…EXTREME anger. This punk beat up my little brother and he wasn't going to get away with it this time!

I tracked this kid down and I told him to meet me in the school parking lot immediately after the game. He must have noticed the rage in my eyes because he never showed up. The next morning, I was out collecting dues for my paper route. After my collections, I treated myself to some candy at the local grocery store. While I was there, I saw this kid shopping with his mother. Again, I challenged him to a fight. This time we were to meet at the lumberyard at 1 pm. Again, he never showed. I spent the next two weeks trying to track him down. I even got myself expelled from school for trying to hit him and instead I hit a teacher by accident. He was avoiding me at all costs and his fear continued to fuel me.

One afternoon while with my mother on her way to pick up the kids from the babysitter, I saw him cross the street heading towards a convenience store. I asked my mother to drop me off, so I could get him. She did so, with no questions asked. Again, skewed parenting was in full effect. Most mothers would not allow their kids to fight, but mine sure didn't seem to mind.

I followed him into the convenience store. He was obviously shocked to see me there. I kept asking him to step outside. He wouldn't. The teenager working at the store knew me from my newspaper route and was standing behind the counter while the kid was leaning against the front side. The teenager encouraged me to hit him in the store. He did so by quietly hitting his one fist into his other hand and then pointing downwards. So I did, I hit him so hard that his head snapped back, cracking a candy dish that was sitting on the countertop. He then ran to the back of the store screaming the entire way. I followed him and maliciously continued my assault. My first hit had been to his left eye and he was holding his hands over it as I continued to hit him wherever I could.

The clerk came back and excitedly commented on how badly I was beating him. I was so pumped up. I eventually stopped for a moment and asked the kid to show me his eye.

He dropped his hands and his eye was swollen and bleeding with all sorts of colors coming through. I still had so much anger that I hit him one last time. I hit that same left eye so hard and quick that he didn't see it coming. Not that he could anyway. The scream that came from him after that punch was music to my ears. I finally got revenge on the bully who had harassed both my baby brother and me. I had become the man that my father envisioned me to be. As I left the store, I saw my mother waiting for me outside. She never saw what happened, nor did she ask. We went home as if nothing happened.

When we arrived home, my father was there as he hadn't made his final departure yet. I told him what happened. He acted as if he didn't care or believed me. I was completely devastated. I thought for sure that this would be the first moment for him to be proud of me. But I got no reaction at all.

A couple of hours later the kid's parents showed up at our house and started to threaten my parents with a lawsuit. They had just returned from the doctor. I broke the bone right below his eye and did some serious damage to the nerves. My father told his parents, "If you want to sue us, no problem. We'll just tell the courts how your kid beat up our other son who is eight years younger than him." That quickly diffused the situation.

My dad got to see firsthand what I had done to the boy, and after they left, he was so excited. He bragged about my actions for the rest of the night. He kept saying, "You see? I made you a man!" I felt like I had finally earned his respect. I would have been happier if he just showed up to support me with my sporting events instead of me becoming some monster, but I took the praise for the brief time that it lasted.

I later heard that the damage to the kid's eye was quite extensive. He had to wear a patch for almost six months as well as having permanent damage to his nerves. There was talk of revenge from his older brother who wanted to come after me but nothing ever came of it. As the years passed, my anger became more refined. I was quick-tempered and sought out trouble. My father started to become more distant and eventually left for good. My mother couldn't control me. She threatened to send me to Boys Town and even sent me away for two straight summers to stay with my grandfather in Houston, Texas. I wanted to be a bully at this point. After all, that was what I was taught. I started hanging around all the tough guys and even found myself bullying my best friend from elementary school simply because the new crowd I hung out with didn't like him.

By the time I was in the eighth grade my father was gone for good and my mother was working two jobs to make ends meet. Because of this, she had hired a full-time babysitter. She was a wonderful Christian woman. I enjoyed her as I would stay with her on the days that I was sick so that my mother didn't have to stay home from work. Not that she would anyway. The babysitter tried very hard to reach out to me. She always told me that I should stop swearing and go to church. She lectured me about my fighting as well. But she managed to do it in such a pleasant way that it wasn't aggravating. She made her talks relatable.

She went so far as to invite me to church once. What an experience that was. The church members were up and screaming for the Lord. It scared me quite a bit, but she made me feel at ease to what I had witnessed. She was so kind and was able to reach me when no one else could. She brought me to tears one time during a conversation that we had about Jesus. Bless her heart, she tried with me. She was very good to my siblings as well. I know all three of them loved her very much. As I reflect on my time with her. God was at work through her to get me to change my ways.

Despite her efforts my fighting ways continued to the point where I got kicked out of school at least twice a year from the eighth grade until I was a junior in high school. In my senior year, I got kicked out four times, but not once for fighting. In my defense, they were for stupid reasons like standing up for what was not right. Two were for minor infractions of singing in the hallway and chewing gum in the library. The third time, I helped organize a sit-in strike. The fourth was for yelling at a basketball game. I will highlight that later. I can guarantee it was due to the fact that I was a little bit of a rebel. You see, if you have the reputation of starting trouble. The radar is locked in on you more than others. So, I guess I had them coming.

I gained my reputation, which didn't take much to get when word had spread about the things I had done.

Despite the notoriety I gained there were guys that wanted to test me or maybe test themselves, who knows. As I went through high school, it seemed all I wanted to do was fight.   I got a rush from it. I didn't care if the other guy was afraid of me or not. The pleasure of inflicting pain on others was all I cared about and it was addicting.

If a fight was starting to brew up I had a habit of getting into their face and talked like a true intimidator. I followed that up by punching myself in the face, which pretty much psyched my opponent out and terrified them from wanting to pursue a fight. I also did it to pump myself up. While I was doing this, I would go so far as to say, " I am so bad, that it is going to take you and me both to whip me". I used this tactic so often that it became my calling card if you will. I would go so far as to brag about how many punches I got in and how few, if any, the other guy got in.

I stated earlier that my mother was working two jobs. She needed to after my father finally left. She also started dating again which left me to take care of the kids in the evening. I tried to cook the best I could for them and took care of the household chores as well. I wasn't acting like a kid. I was being forced to grow up and take on adult responsibilities. However, there was true love in the house shared between my siblings and me. During such a crazy time, you would think my mother would have become more lovable to us but her priorities revolved around the men she was dating. In today's world, she would have been in major trouble with the current laws concerning child abuse and neglect. My father would be in a lot of trouble as well for the abuse.

I always wondered what my mother possibly saw in some of the men she used to date. Most of them were much older than her and looked like life had worn them out. Even though my father abused us, there was a psychological effect that he had on me. I always felt like the men my mother dated could never measure up to him. To this day, I still find that kind of twisted. She finally met a man when she was working her night job as a waitress at a local bar and grill. He was a retired Air Force man who was fourteen years older than her. He had six kids of his own; with his youngest son just one year older than me. Anyway, my mother and he hit it off quite well. So well in fact, that they decided to move in together at his home. The way they went about it was so wrong.

After I spent that weekend with my grandma, she brought me home on Sunday afternoon. Since I had a key to the place, she didn't wait to see whether anyone else was home as long as I got in alright. To my surprise, my mom and the kids had moved out with no idea of where they could be. No note, no nothing. Gone! So I had to wait a while for my grandma to get back home to call her and tell her that I was all alone and that there was no food in the house. Before my grandma could come back and get me, I received a phone call from my mom's new boyfriend. He was telling me that I had no choice but to move in with them. Though I argued with him and told him of my dislike of him and this entire situation. He replied that he was given instructions by my mom to have his four boys kick my butt.

My mother had told him that I had become unruly and that was the only way to straighten me out. Again, here is parenting at its finest. I was a product of my environment and yet it was my fault. My grandma finally came back and took me to her house. Which prompted an argument between her and my mom later that evening?

Needless to say, my new relationship got off to a poor start. I hated my mom's boyfriend and everything he represented. Ultimately, I had no choice but to move into his house with the rest of my family. Along with the move came a new town and a new school. My fighting skills would have to come in handy now. Being the new kid in school is rough and I had to prove myself all over again. I hated this change so much that I got to the point where I hated life. I didn't care about anything anymore. I hung out with the wrong crowd. I went to parties and even did some vandalizing. I started smoking cigarettes and completely gave up on all my sports.

Chapter 2

Growing Up

My mom and her boyfriend announced that they were getting married at the end of the school year. I still didn't approve of him and thought he was extremely phony. I didn't want him to be my step-father. I surely was not going to call him "Dad", either. I refused to live in that house with them being married so it was arranged somehow through my aunt, my mom's sister that I was to go live with my biological father. I preferred that option despite how abusive he was towards me.

My mother and new step-father had the wedding and reception at their house. My grandmother and aunt attended and I ended up going home with them that night. Later that weekend, my father picked me up at my grandmother's house to take me to his place in northern Nebraska. It was very strange because he was nice to me. Maybe in his mind, he thought the fact that I wanted to live with him implied that he was the better parent.

My time at his house started fairly well because my father was finally acting like a dad. For the first time in my life, I enjoyed being with him. We spent quality time together. He taught me how to ride a motorcycle and took me fishing quite often. We got along so well. It truly seemed like he had changed for the better. He would go to work and then come home immediately afterward. He didn't go to the bars and didn't drink at home. It was like he was happier for whatever reason.

He had a live-in girlfriend. This was the same girlfriend that he had for many years. She had a couple of her own kids living there as well as a child that she and my father had together. It was as if I had a new family. Her oldest son was the closest to my age. He was two years older than me. He was easy to get along with and he helped ease the tension between my father and me. He could get my father to laugh at his stupid jokes and impressions. He built within me the courage to speak to my father like a kid should be able to do.

That summer was one of my most enjoyable ones to date. At the end of the season, the oldest son needed to go back to Colorado where he lived with his dad. So

my father, his girlfriend and I drove him out there. After
we dropped him off, we visited the mountains and had a
nice vacation. I'll never forget it. One night we stayed
at a cabin resort outside of Estes Park. It was getting
late and I was asked to go to the car and get the
luggage out of the trunk. With flashlight in hand, I went.
As I was trying to put the key into the lock I noticed a big
bear print on the trunk. It scared me so much that I
dropped the flashlight and ran back into the cabin. My
father got a kick out of it, but he decided we didn't need
the luggage until morning.

When we returned to Nebraska, things between my
father and I changed for the worse very quickly.   His
girlfriend tried her best to cause problems between him
and me. I think she noticed the bond he and I were
developing especially with her son out of the picture and
got jealous because her kids weren't getting the same
attention.

My father asked her to take me shopping for school
clothes. The only problem was that everything I picked
out she told me my father wouldn't like. After a full day
of shopping and aggravation, we came back with

nothing. All of the clothes that I wanted were Levi jeans and button-up shirts. These were the exact type of clothes that my father wore. When he asked me why I didn't have any new school clothes, she interrupted by saying, "Everything I picked out for him, he didn't like. He was a royal pain!". Though my father and I were getting closer, I still didn't feel comfortable enough telling him the truth about what happened. So, I simply ignored the situation.

It was these types of behaviors that she and her daughters shared that killed the relationship between my father and me. The straw that broke the camel's back was when they told my father about a marijuana plant that was stashed away in the attic. The thing about this plant was that it had been picked earlier in the summer, by the oldest son. I guess he forgot about it or decided to leave it for the next summer. Well, I ended up being blamed for it and my father was so furious that he beat me within an inch of my life. After that evening, I swore that I would get revenge on his girlfriend and her daughters. I also vowed never to allow myself to get beat like that again. I told myself there will be a time when he wished he never touched me.

Shortly after that, my father had kicked me out of his house. He took me back to live with my mom and step-father. The reception was warm, but I wasn't happy. My step-father did everything he could to try to make me feel comfortable. Like I said earlier, I thought he was phony. By then I was beginning my freshman year in high school and once again I got in the wrong crowd and continued becoming a deviant. I was smoking cigarettes, drinking beer, and going to parties regularly. What was crazy about all of this, was that I was allowed. No one tried to stop me or tell me I couldn't. I didn't care about school and even considered dropping out.

This was a weird and different time in my life. I didn't care about sports, myself, or anything else. The sad thing about it all is you would think I could talk to my mom. After all, she is my mother. But she was unapproachable. When I reached out to my grandmothers, she got jealous. To the point, she was intercepting my letters to my grandmother in Virginia both incoming and outgoing. Another crime she could have been punished for. As well as she would not let me call my grandma who lived close by. Of course, the trials and tribulations kept coming. One time it came in the form of the town bully. He was a dropout that worked at a local gas station. One night I was at the town bar which allowed kids to hang out until 0 pm. My friends and I went there to play pool, foosball, and grabbed a bite to eat. After hanging out for a bit, one of my friends told me that the guy was waiting for me outside and wanted to fight. Truthfully, I wasn't in the mood but he wasn't leaving until we fought it out. So, I went outside to fight him and let me tell you, did we fight. We knocked each other senseless. We hit each other's heads against the brick walls, the sidewalk, you name it. If there was a foreign object to use on one another, they got used. It was a very bloody fight. Thank God, an older gentleman finally broke up the fight. I was relieved because we were both exhausted but neither of us wanted to accept defeat.

This town was a rough one for me. No matter how well I fought, I continually had to keep proving myself. I was an outsider and considered a drug addict because of the people I hung out with. I was jumped by two or more guys on a couple of separate occasions. All that did was spark more anger and made me sharpen my

fighting skills in case I had to fight more than one guy
again. It came in handy as there was one particular
fight where I was outnumbered by four guys and came
out victorious. I called that my "Coming of Age" fight. I
felt indestructible.

Because I had to fight more than one guy at a time on
occasion. Do you have any idea what that did to my
confidence? I would make comments that I was so bad,
that it took more than one guy to whip me. Just like
when I would psyche out an opponent by hitting myself
in the face. I would say "I am so bad, that it will take all
of us to kick my butt, let me get started".

After my freshman year, my parents were told they
had to move because of me. I had gotten into yet
another fight. This time it was because I had beat up
the kid living across the street. I can't remember exactly
why I did it, I just remember I did. My parents owned a
mobile home with an addition built-on. It was located in
a great spot, right next to a lake. Even though the
house was theirs, the property was not. So they were
told to vacate.

During that summer we moved thirteen miles away to a new town. All I could think about was here I go again, a new kid in a new town. But I was going to make the best of this new chapter in my life. I had spoken to my step-dad about getting back into sports. He thought it was a good idea. He felt I could use it as an outlet to release some of my pent up anger. Not only that, but we were also moving close to where we used to live when I was younger. I felt I could fit in better as I would know some of the other kids. I was excited about a new school, a new home, and a fresh start.

I started playing football that year. Even though I was a little undersized, my heart was into the game. I ended up starting on the junior varsity squad at defensive end. I had a really good season. I eventually ended up starting my next two seasons at that position on the varsity squad. I found myself being accepted by kinder and nicer people. I was starting to fit in with the popular crowd.

Just like any small town there is always going to be someone to test you. There was this one guy on the football team that didn't seem to like me much. My first encounter with him was after school before the homecoming football game. I was sitting in a restaurant when he confronted me about sitting in "His" booth. I told him he could have it when I was done eating. He looked at me sarcastically and said, "I will see you later". He didn't start a scene there because his parents owned the place. Later that night during the game, he went out of his way to always bump into me along the sidelines, giving me dirty looks and whatever else he could to annoy me.

After the game, I was invited to a keg party. I went along with my new girlfriend and another couple. Everything was going fine until I found myself standing at the keg pouring myself a beer and here Mr. Football comes. "So you think you're tough?" he said. I replied, "I never said that". "He said, "apparently so because you wear that wrestling t-shirt". This was a shirt I wore under my shoulder pads. It was an old wrestling t-shirt that I acquired during the years. I told him the shirt was nothing more than a shirt. He told me to follow him outside, which of course I did. What was strange is I thought we would have had some followers, but no one came along.

We ended up standing in between two cars just staring at each other. He got closer to me and started snarling and growling. He wanted me to hit him. He got right up to my face and I refused to flinch. He was saying things to me in hopes that I would take a swing at him. Again, I didn't move, I just stood there staring him down, just like he stared at me. He then reached his arm around my neck like a chokehold. He drew me in close to him and said, "Kid, stick with me and you will go places." He was impressed despite his size over me that I would not back down from him. We ended up being the closest of friends. It was nice; he was considered the toughest guy in school. That helped my reputation and adjustment because we were friends.

I would go on to a somewhat normal adolescent lifestyle. I had my shares of ups and downs, successes, and failures, but for the most part, a very memorable time. I was extremely active in sports. I tried my hand at a school play, I was part of the school newspaper and on the yearbook staff. I had my share of girlfriends and close buddies. I wrestled every year and went out for track, just to quit as I hated running in circles.

During those days I never really had to fight much, though I still did. Mostly to defend the honor of a friend in case they were wronged. I had a reputation of being mean and at times I felt I had to make sure people remembered it. I still had some challengers but then you have that type of reputation, for the most part, people don't want to get on our bad side.

I had made a promise to my step-dad that during my senior year that I would not get kicked out of school for fighting. My grades were pretty good and there was talk that I may go to college. The first time I got kicked out was for singing "Lola" by the Kinks while I was walking down the hallway. You have to understand before my senior year. The school used to play the local rock station over the intercom and we could hear it in between classes. Depending on the teacher we were allowed to listen to it during class. It was nice; we had a newly built school and had some perks that came with it. Our new principal put a stop to that. Because I was missing the music, I decided to make my own. That cost me a one-day suspension.

This principal changed a lot of things. He did so drastically that someone mentioned that we ought to have a sit-in strike. When I got wind of that, I got together with a couple of my rowdy friends, five in all. We made it happen and quickly. It was talked about on Monday and went off between the second and third periods on Tuesday. We asked for all students to not go to their third-period class and to gather in the commons area.   Believe it or not, we got some results. The principal tried to put a stop to it, but he was laughed at. The superintendent got involved and through him, we formed a unity council. It was made up of two representatives from every grade seventh through twelfth. We were able to sit down and visit with him to voice our concerns. The next day, everything was back to normal. So, we thought. During the second period, one of my buddies got called to the principal's office. When he returned to gather his things, he had informed us that he had been suspended five days for organizing the strike.

It seemed it would be a matter of time before the rest of us would get the boot. The entire day went by and not one of us got called to the office. The day after that the remaining of us went to the principal's office and asked him 'Why not us?" He replied by saying that we were not the organizers and that we got suckered into it. We told him that we were just as responsible and that we should get kicked out as well. Thus, the principal called every one of our parents and told them what was going to happen.

After we were expelled, most of us went to my house and stayed there all day. I think a couple of my friends were not looking forward to going home. Eventually, my step-dad came home, and since he was the one that was called as opposed to my mom, he knew what was going on. He commended all of us for standing up for what we believed in. He told the others that they must have been special to me. Because I was trying so hard to go to college and that I put that in jeopardy to stand up for what was right. I began to admire him a little more at that time. He also earned respect from my friends.

I said earlier that I got kicked out of school for yelling at a basketball game. This is how it went down. Those of us who did not play basketball organized a cheering section we called the "bleacher creatures". We harassed the opposing team and got on the referees whenever we had a foul called against us.

One of the girls that played on our team was very good. She was so good she could beat most guys one on one. She was closing in on the state all-time scoring record. This particular night she was just four points away. Though I had not gone to school that day due to a scratchy throat I wanted to attend the game. My parents made me promise if I went to school the next day I could go. They knew how much I wanted to see her break the record.

Since it was an away game there were not as many of our students in attendance. During the game, there was a bad call. So, the bleacher creatures started yelling the "BS" word. A couple of faculty members who were attending frowned at us. They started making up a list of students that were yelling the profanities. Wouldn't you know it, my name was on that list? Mind you, my girlfriend who was there with me had a reputation of being a good girl and her name wasn't on the list despite the fact she sat right next to me. Now remember I could barely talk, but apparently, I could scream.

The next day I was called to the office to be informed that I was being suspended for five days. I was furious. I went home to call my step-dad. He was so upset that he left work early to go to see the principal. He asked me to meet him there. Remember he was a retired air force sergeant but now he was working at a grain elevator. His job required him to walk in manure and rotten grain. It was so bad it was a nightly chore to clean his boots every day before he left work.

When we got to the principal's office, he was steaming mad. He accused the principal of trying to ruin my chances of going to college and that he was being unprofessional by holding a personal grudge against me. He also stated that there was no way that I could have yelled the profanities at the basketball game because he had first-hand knowledge of my condition. I could barely talk let alone yell. I was still having a hard time talking. So, while my step-dad was yelling at the principal he brought out his pocket knife and pointed it towards the principal. It probably scared the principal to death. When he wasn't pointing it, he was using it to scrap all of the crap off his boots and letting it fall onto the carpet.

All this time I was amazed by how my stepdad went to bat for me. Just four short years ago he and I couldn't stand each other and now here we are side by side standing up for what was right. My step-dad and I had reached a pinnacle in our relationship. We were father and son. Better yet we were friends.

During my senior year, I experienced true grief when my dad's father passed away. He was a great man. A lot better than my father. I didn't see him as much as my other grandparents, but when I did, we bonded very well. It was this grandpa that gave me my first car. He called my step-dad when I was a sophomore and asked him if it was okay. My step-dad agreed that it was a nice gesture. Since the car needed a new water pump, we had to tow it home. It was a 1964 Ford Falcon station wagon. It was white with a red interior. It was the perfect color for a Husker fan. I wish I could say the car itself was perfect but it was far from it. Don't get me wrong I was very appreciative of his gift. After I replaced the water pump and got it running, it would only go so fast. I used to joke it wouldn't go fifty-five miles per hour, downhill with a gust of wind. But it got me from point A to point B. That was the most important thing. It was just a little slower than most and it was mine.

The day of his passing was hard for me because that same day I received a letter informing me of my scholarship to play football. It wasn't a full ride. But hey, I'm going to go play college football. He would have been one of the first people I would have called. I know he would have been very excited for me.

Things between my step-dad and I kept getting better. We had our good days and our bad. When it was good it was really good. We had some nice male bonding moments. We spent time just talking about life. It was then that he showed me he wanted to be instrumental during my adolescent years. He shaped quite a bit of the character I have today. He instilled in me discipline and hard work. He taught me how to be organized and most importantly how to have fun with life.

For instance, there was a time when he asked me to do a couple of chores on a Saturday morning while he would be gone. I got up, messed around the house, and did absolutely nothing until the Nebraska football game started airing over the radio. He came home and walked into my room and asked me why I hadn't done my chores. I told him, "I would, as soon as the game is over". He walked over to my stereo and shut it off. He said "Business before pleasure. So, I got up and did my chores. It took me all of thirty minutes to finish. For punishment, I wasn't allowed to finish listening to the game as well as I had to stay home that night. It was a very tough lesson for a die-hard Husker fan to digest. Later on, he came back into my room and explained to me why such a harsh punishment for a small crime. If this would have happened a couple of years earlier, I would have thrown a fit. But I was growing up and our relationship was getting stronger. I took his words to heart to the tune that I live my life like that today. A life lesson if you will.

He was cool with me in a lot of areas. He allowed me to drink at the house. He trusted me to take his truck to parties when he knew I would be drinking. Since he

was a lifetime member and post commander of the
Veterans of Foreign War, I would go there with him as
well. There he would order a whiskey and coke and
then a regular coke. He would let me drink the cocktails
while he would drink and pretend to drink the soda along
with his beer. I can tell you this. The main reason I
went with him to the V.F.W. club was so I could be his
designated driver. Think about that. I was given drinks
by a man so he could drink more than me so he would
get home safe.

When I did drive home, we usually took the dirt roads
home. I knew of a four-way stop at the top of this hill.
As I got closer to the intersection, I would shut the
headlights off to see if I saw any other headlights.
When I didn't, I would blow through the crossing, all
along scaring him to death. You see we did have fun
together. If you want to call that fun. I enjoyed it.

He also had no problem if I decided to throw a party
at the house. There were times when he would even
buy the keg for me as long as my friends and I paid for
it. He didn't mind the parties. I think they made him feel
young again because he was very flirtatious with all the

girls. He was also very cautious with my friends when it came to someone driving home. He didn't want anyone to get hurt. He made arrangements for someone to get home or he would drive them home himself.

It wasn't smooth sailing all the time. Every once in a while after he had been drinking, we would want to get into a fight. He finally realized that I was too young and too strong for him to attempt to scrap with me. Because my admiration for him was rowing, I didn't want any confrontation with him either. He never tried to impose fighting on me like my real father did but, he did not discourage me either.

He and mom were not necessarily the best of parents. After all, we could drink, smoke and cuss. But they did have simple house rules. We needed to be home for dinner, we had a curfew on school nights and we better get our chores done. When I asked my step-dad what time he wanted me to be home on weekend nights, he would simply reply "Let your conscience be your guide". I respected him for that. It showed that he trusted me. I think as time grew they felt they had to have some sort of discipline in the household. Maybe because they were gone so much or they felt as adults someone had to be in charge.

For the most part, my siblings and I pretty much did whatever we wanted. Even though we had some rules we weren't taught anything of good value. I guess I could say as bad as that may sound it was much better than the road I was heading down if my parents had stayed together.

With all the fights I had gotten into over the years, there was still that one fight I always wanted and never got. That was with my father. While I was in the Army, my baby brother had gone off to live with our father because of the turmoil going on at the house between my mom and step-dad. It was the early stages of their divorce. My brother just felt like he had to get out.

I came home on leave from the Army for the holidays. At the time my youngest sister was the only one living at home, though she had already graduated from high school. My oldest sister had gotten married and was living in another state. The youngest was heartbroken that my brother would not be home for Christmas. So, along with her future husband, we went to get our baby brother. When we got to the town where he lived, we still had no idea where the house was located. Since it was such a small town it didn't take much to ask around and find out. When we did find our brother, he was excited and was very willing to go home with us. There was one catch though...we had to ask our father if we could take him. We waited as long as we could for him to come home. Finally, we decided to go to the local bar, which is where we found him. Go figure.

We all went back to his house and chatted for a while. During the conversation, my sister and her fiancé told him about their wedding plans. Our father asked, "Don't you think you should ask my permission first?" I stood up and said, "Who are you to be asking such a thing?" I went on to state that he ran out on us, and if they need anyone's permission it was mine and they had it. So, he responded. "You're the tough guy now, the big football player and wrestler." "If you're so tough, do you want to fight?" I was so ready! I was going to get my chance of sweet redemption. My sister begged me not to fight him. After all, we were only there to get our little brother. She felt that if there was to be a fight, it might jeopardize our mission. She said I would get my day with him just another time. So in the spirit of keeping her happy, I let it go. Little did we know that would be the last time we would see him alive. Looking back on that, I am glad that we didn't fight. As bad as I wanted it, I can almost guarantee you one of us probably wouldn't have walked away from it.

It seemed like my entire life was surrounded by fighting. I couldn't get away from it, no matter what I did. There were times I felt it was a problem, but I wasn't going to admit it out loud. I had people that cared for me and didn't like it. But I just couldn't escape it, though there were times I did the right thing by not fighting, I just didn't do it often enough.

Before I went off to the Army. I had befriended this wonderful family. The father was a retired police officer. He was six-foot-four and close to three hundred pounds. He was not one to mess with. After his retirement, he dabbled in some side jobs to bring home money. One of them was to work security at local high school football games. One night, I had gone with him, and as we were leaning against the fence watching the crowd. He spotted Tom Osborne, the head football coach at The University of Nebraska. Coach Osborne had worked his way up to the highest point in the bleachers, sitting there all by himself. I finally worked up the nerve to go ask him for an autograph. When I approached him, he told me he was there to scout a recruit and he didn't want any distractions. I replied as much as I appreciated that I was just a month or so from going into the Army and wasn't sure if I would ever see him again. He smiled, gave me his autograph, and wished me well.

After the game, I started to head back to the car. On my way, I came across these two guys that were fighting. I felt it was my duty to stop it; after all, I was there with a security guard. So, here I am trying to stop this fight, not being too successful. They were wrapped up like wrestlers. When I would get one arm loose to work on another, they would go back to the same old thing. All of a sudden, here comes these extra pairs of hands to help me. It was Coach Osborne. Let me tell you, he gave these guys such a lecture that he had me standing at attention and I wasn't fighting.

I only wished his speech had a better impact on me that I stopped fighting once and for all. I needed someone like Coach Osborne in my life. Someone who I admired and looked up to. I needed someone to tell me how stupid I looked and how wrong it was to fight. Not just once but consistently. After all, I had been programmed to do it. I think because of that I developed more anger and resentment in my life. I was jealous of the fact that others came from such loving families. It made me sick to my stomach. I always wondered why I wasn't fortunate enough to have such a wonderful childhood like others around me.

I spent years continuing to fight. The truth is that I could write an entire book about my fighting escapades. Having been a part of over 150 fights in my lifetime. I look back now and am not pleased or proud of how I behaved. But many lessons are learned the hard way. Thus, my journey through life evolves.

Chapter 3

Confusion

There is an element of my fighting that I would like to mention. I can't think of a single time where I had not been drinking. Just as fighting was a part of my life, so was drinking. I distinctly remember my first beer. A friend of mine was sleeping over one evening. Even though she wouldn't be home that night to monitor us, my mom bought us a six-pack of beer. We thought we were so cool that night. We called friends bragging and rubbing it in. Despite how cool we thought we were, we didn't finish off all of it. It was pretty much two beers each and done. It took us roughly ninety minutes to do that. We were still the coolest that night or at least in our little world.

Just like fighting, I got into trouble with my drinking. Eventually, the two of them would land me in jail. The first time I was arrested, I was nineteen years old. I was pulled over for turning on my spotlights, which were mounted on the roll bar of my pick up truck. They were so bright that they blinded the oncoming traffic, which happened to be the police. When they pulled me over, I had close to a case of beer in my truck. They arrested me for a minor in possession. They also tried repeatedly to charge me with driving under the influence. But every time I blew into the breathalyzer I passed with little to no reading. I am not encouraging anyone on how to beat a breathalyzer test. But I had heard if you plugged the hole of the tube with your tongue and blew around the tube, it would not detect any reading. Since then I have heard that they have got wise to that method and have a completely different test now. Regardless, it would be just a matter of time before I would get hit with that charge as well. I got arrested for DUI at the age of twenty-two.

I wasn't arrested for fighting until I was twenty-nine. That incident shocked me. It wasn't that big of a fight, at least not to me. I did hurt the guy, but I had done far worse to others. I was thinking to myself. Why? And Why now? Could it be that it was different in Florida than Nebraska? Was the guy the type to call the police on every little thing? Back home when two guys got into a fight. No one called the police. Even if you lost, it was a life lesson. Just don't lose again or take it like a man.

Then it hit me. It was karma. I had done so much to so many that it finally caught up with me. Yes, I had been drinking even though it was just a small amount.

My lawyer tried that it was in self-defense. That I retaliated from being hit first, not to mention that I was defending the honor of someone I care deeply for. He went so far as to compare me to our founding fathers. A hero, if you like. When the judge made his decision, he told me that it was a state law that if someone hits you, you can only retaliate using the same or less force. So, if I was hit. I should have stopped with one punch. Not beat the snot out of the guy. He also said though he admired me for my actions but he had to abide by the law. He further said that I could go to jail for one year, but since it was my first offense, he was only going to give me ninety days. I think he liked what I stood up for by his comments. So off to county jail I went and I was released after sixty days. The worst of it was that I lost my job as a retail manager. My boss didn't look at me the same as the judge. No, worries as I got another manager job fairly quickly.

As I look back on that incident and what was said.
The judge was also considering me a hero. He was no
different than my buddies that patted me on the back or
bought me a beer for being victorious. I was being
praised. Was this my calling? Was there fuel being
poured onto the fire?

If it is possible to say anything good about my
fighting, it would be that I often found myself fighting for
others. Just like when I beat up that kid for hurting my
brother. I fought for friends and other family members
that I cared for. The incident that finally got me thrown
in jail was because I was defending the honor of those
that I love very much. It's funny but I can remember my
oldest sister, asking me on a couple of occasions to
beat someone up for her because she got her feelings
hurt. Just like my father taught me. If someone messes
with you, you beat them up and they won't mess with
you again. If you hurt someone dear to me, you were
going to pay the price.

I didn't think I had a drinking problem. I was just a
young kid having the time of my life. Besides, my logic
was that people with egos don't have problems. I know,

it sounds crazy but that was my mentality back then. After I had been arrested for my minor in possession charge, the courts wanted to know if I met the criteria to attend an Alcoholics Anonymous class. The lady I had to meet with that morning asked me ten questions. I answered yes, to only one of them. That question was, "Do you ever feel a need to drink?" When I said "Yes", told her it was usually when I got home from a hard day of work. I liked to relax, watch the news, read the paper, and drink a cold beer. This lady told me that I was considered an alcoholic because I was dependent on it.

As I looked at this huge coffee cup she had sitting on her desk. I asked her "Why do you need that big cup of coffee?" I followed up with comments along the line of her needing the coffee to get going in the morning like I needed the beer to unwind at night. I told her that I wasn't going to go to her ridiculous AA class. If they needed to throw me in jail for that, then go ahead and do so. Thankfully for me, I did not get jail time or the AA class. I can guarantee you one thing. She got rid of that coffee cup.

A little side note here. Over the years I have often thought of how good our judicial system is. As I look back, I can say that it has its flaws. Over ten years, two different states, on two different occasions had an opportunity to help shape someone like me to not repeat. But because of the antics by both my lawyer and me, even though they were both first-time offenses, I got off pretty easy. In reality, I feel like I manipulated the system if you please. It just makes me wonder what their priorities or mindsets are when someone like me or even worse enters the system. Are they trying to rehabilitate or are they a money-making machine like any other business?

Drinking for me seemed normal. After all, I had my first beer when I was in the eighth grade. Before my mom and step-dad were married. I was a free bird. This means I pretty much did what I wanted. I went to parties, started smoking cigarettes, and drank beer a lot. At some stage in my adolescent years it became acceptable that I could drink anytime I wanted to at home.

One thing I am proud of is that I never got into drugs. There was something about it that never appealed to me. Maybe it was the spaced-out look people got when they were high, the smell of it, or just the fact I wasn't a fan of smoking. When I did smoke cigarettes, it was usually related to my drinking meaning I didn't do it all the time. I think I smoked more for the reason of trying to look tough or grown-up. I never liked it, I just did it. I couldn't inhale the smoke. My friends noticed that and would give me a hard time about it.

I said before that my childhood was not filled with love. I became misconstrued about what love truly was. I can honestly say that I cannot remember one time where my parents gave me a hug or a kiss or told me that they loved me. I guess it wasn't in their nature. It wasn't until the weekends that I spent with my grandma that I realized what I was missing at home. She was such a sweet woman, always kind, and loving. She always gave me a kiss goodnight and told me she loved me. It hit my heart so hard that I would sometimes cry myself to sleep. I was confused as to why there was always so much violence, abuse, and fear at home and at grandma's house; it was full of peace and love.

It was during my junior year in high school when I first heard the words "I love you" directed toward me in my house. It was my step-dad that said it. Of course, he was drinking at the time and it was hard for me to believe him. I figured he was just running off at the mouth. It just didn't feel right. I'm not sure if it was that I didn't want to believe him. Under the circumstances without ever hearing it at home before, it was a very hard thing to handle or get used to.

Do you know how they say that your cousin is usually your first true friend? Well, I had a cousin on my father's side that I was very close to. We were the same age and enjoyed the same things. We liked to spend weekends together as much as possible. But we had to do it mostly at his house. His father who had married into my family did not accept the ways of our household, especially early on when my father was around. He would never allow his son to stay at my house. He thought it was an unhealthy environment knowing how my father could get drunk and start on one of his tirades. I know this quite well, as it always came up in conversation whenever I stayed over. He knew how close my cousin and I were and that we would want to spend time together as much as possible. If he had some free time to give us a fun weekend he would. I think he made every effort to get us together. He wanted me to spend time with them knowing the situation at my house and wanted me to get away as much as possible for my good.

My cousin and his father had a great relationship. You could tell it was a relationship built from love. They did things together just as a father and son should do. He would take my cousin fishing and hunting as well as he was always a part of his extracurricular activities. Football, boy scouts, whatever it was, he was there. What got me was they would tell each other "I love you". That kind of freaked me out. One guy saying it to another, but you could tell they had something special. I didn't know it at the time but, I was jealous of what they had and envied my cousin.

To give you an idea of comparison, I went hunting with my father once and had to sit in the truck as he walked the fields for pheasant. When he took me fishing, he got upset because I caught seven catfish while he didn't catch one. It upset him so much I was never asked to go again. Isn't that ridiculous to be mad at your child for having success at something? But that was how things went in my life.

I played baseball, football, and wrestled a little bit as a kid. I loved my sports. My father never once came to a game to cheer me on or wished me well before a game. He never played ball with me in the yard. He never had a clue as to whether I was even good at the sports I played or not. He never asked if I won or lost.

I loved my sports so much that it became my scapegoat. When I was a little boy, I took an old tire and placed it on the back of the dog house. From there I built up a pitching mound and would throw my baseball into the tire. If I pitched the ball through the tire, it was a strike. If I hit the tire, it was a ball and if I missed the tire it was a hit. If I missed the doghouse completely, I gave up a home run. I would also practice catching fly balls by throwing the ball up as high and as far away as I could so I could chase it down and catch it. I would also throw a tennis ball up against the outside wall of the house and practice my grounders.

I did the same with football. I would pretend to snap the ball to myself, then throw it to myself and even fall down as if I were being tackled. I did so much on my own. I used my imagination and had fun with it. I had no choice, my father wasn't around much and if he was, he was either drunk or yelling. But he was never there for me. Because I was so young, I wasn't allowed to leave the yard. Thinking about it now, I probably could have gone off and my parents would have never noticed I was gone.

When I was eight years old, I became one of the happiest boys in the world as I finally had a baby brother. As much as I enjoyed it, I think it took me a while to realize that I would have to wait to have him as a playmate. I can promise you as we got older and he could play ball, we did. I taught him everything I knew and enjoyed our time together. I think I gave him the father figure that I lacked as a child.

When my step-dad and I discussed the option of me getting back into the game. He told me he would support me no matter what as long as I kept my grades up. To my surprise, he stayed true to that. He went to my football games and wrestling matches. What was funny is that he didn't have a clue of how the games were to be played or what the rules were. My mom had to teach him what first and ten meant as well as many other things. However, he became involved, and that's what mattered most to me. After my games or matches, we would go home, have a couple of beers and talk about my evening. He asked me to educate him about my sports so that he could give me better words of encouragement or tell me good job for a well done deed. I truly feel that it was sports that gave us solid ground to what would eventually be a great relationship.

The summer after my sophomore year, he decided we were going to build an addition on to the house. Each day he would give me a particular job to do. Sometimes he would have to show me exactly how he wanted it done. Other times, he left it up to me to figure things out on my own. Each day when he got home from work, he would inspect the job and give me instructions for the next day. Before I knew it, I had pretty much built the entire addition all by myself. The only things I needed help with was pouring the foundation, laying the bricks and putting up the trusses.

Everything else I pretty much did on my own to include the electrical work. If you know me at all, I hate messing with electricity.

In this addition, we added a laundry room, family room with a wood burning stove, a bar area, and a bedroom which ended up being mine for doing the work. In the bar area, we had a full-size refrigerator that as stocked all of the time with beer and it was at my disposal anytime. I was never held accountable for it and it was easy for me because I had to walk past the bar to get to my bedroom. I also think my step-dad probably thought I deserved a beer now and then. He gave me some pretty big tasks at times and to a man who does physical labor. Nothing goes down better than an ice-cold beer.

He ended up being a really good father to me for the most part. I was still confused in a lot of areas of our relationship. I still couldn't understand how you could tell someone how much you care for them one day and want to fight them the next. I think he always wanted to do what was right. But I also believe he didn't know how to himself.

To give you an example, one Sunday afternoon I went motorcycle riding with some friends. When I got home and went into my bedroom. I found my step-dad sitting on my bed while holding a beer in his hand. You could tell it wasn't his first one. He asked me why my clothes were not put away. My mother had done laundry while I was out. She folded up my clothes and placed them on my bed for me to take care of. I told him that I just got home and that I would get right on it. As I tried to walk past him to get to my clothes, he jumped up and hit me. I retaliated by hitting him back and ended up knocking him through my sliding closet doors. The next thing I know my oldest step-brother came to is aide. The two of us got into a fight, which was one of many between us.

Now you can see somewhat of the type of life I lived. There was good and bad behavior but never stability. My step-dad had six kids of his own, four boys and two girls. With my mother, he accepted four more kids. I could remember when he would talk about his family to his buddies. He bragged that he had such a big family. "I got ten kids". He would say with his chest out like a gorilla with pride. I truly believe he was. He did have a

kind heart when he wanted to. But as far as us being a
family, I never saw it.   His kids never really accepted
my mother or us. We were anything but a family. You
could say there was jealousy, a little bit of hatred and
resentment, but not a family.

In the beginning, I think they wanted to accept us
probably more for the benefit of their dad. Despite my
feelings of the relationship my mother was in and
resenting everything affiliated with it. I could tell their
thoughts were similar to mine as they did not try to
reach out to me.   They were the exact opposite. Maybe
they were threatened, who knows what was going on in
their minds. I could say that for all of them except the
oldest daughter. You could tell she was cut from a
different cloth, she looked at everything with an open
heart. She didn't party, held a job for a long period, as
well as being married with a son. But the best thing
about her was she was a good Christian woman.

Occasionally on Sundays, she and her family would
come to visit, after church naturally. We would gather
around the dining room table, play rummy, eat snacks,
and enjoy each other's company. All the while she

watched her dad and controlled him to the best of her ability from drinking so much. She would use her son as leverage by saying "You don't want him to see you this way". It worked for the most part. When it was just her family, it was a nice time. Not so much when the others came to visit.

They would rebel against her and her ways as well as everyone else's. It was at times like this that I would think that they didn't respect their dad. They were only out for what they could get free beer, food, or whatever. The visits only lasted for so long. There ended up being turmoil between the two families. It's a safe bet to tell you that my mom had a lot to do with that.

My mom and step-dad married in 1978. Split up sometime in the late 1980s and divorced shortly after. I cannot speculate on everything that happened as I was not living at home at the time. But I was aware of some of my mom's shenanigans and felt sorry for what she put my step-father through. As I look back at those times. I realized he was a simple man, loved his family, and was susceptible to being hurt. I think the divorce from my mother increased his drinking so much that it caused him to have a heart attack. He passed away in 1994. When my mom and he divorced, I took his side which I think surprised some. Over the years I started to see who he really was. Sometimes I wish he were alive to not only help me with my problems, or me with his. Also, for him to see how I turned out, knowing he would tell me he is pleased.

He took us, four kids, into his home and loved us to the best of his ability. My siblings had a better time with him than I did but he is truly missed by all of us. I wish I would have had a chance to tell him I loved him. Even though we had our fair share of problems. I want to thank him for putting up with me and guiding me along as much as he did and for being kind enough to accept our mom with us four kids. I know one thing, as much of a problem as I was for him and him for me, we bonded, we trusted and cared for one another I stood up for him in many ways. One night when I was still living at home, they had a night of drinking. Of course, that leads to a fight which was normal for them. My step-dad, as usual, kissed a girl on the cheek. He kissed all the girls. Well, my mom hit him with a set of keys that she placed between each of her fingers. She raked him pretty good across the face leaving some nasty marks on his cheek. I jumped all over her for that. Seriously, everything he had done for her. This is how she repaid him. He wasn't perfect by no means, but he took us out of a bad situation and made our lives better. This is what happens when a couple goes to a bar or drinks a lot. It is inevitable.

Chapter 4

Lost In Love

I am not a psychiatrist (obviously), but I am pretty sure I used my love of sports to make up shortcomings in my life. My sports were about the only place where I felt accepted and loved. When I played little league baseball, I was on a team that won three championships in a row. Back then they tried to keep the same teams together year after year. Anyway, we were good. I started at third base and I was also the lead-off hitter. I was pretty fast. I wasn't much of a home run hitter, but I could put the ball into play. What was nice is that after each win, we would get in the back of somebody's truck and be driven to A&W to get a free root beer. On the way there we would chant, "We're number one!" and things of that nature. I was a part of something special. I soaked it in as much as I could.

From there I got involved with wrestling and football. In Nebraska, it is almost impossible to live there and not love football. People take football very seriously there. You probably have heard that some think of it as a religion. It is so extreme that life pretty much comes to a stop while the game is on. Back in the day radio was the only way to know what was going on with the games. You could go shopping anywhere you wanted and the game would be aired over the stores' intercom. You could go to the mall from store to store and not miss a play. You knew when we scored because everyone in the store cheered. Through this team, I was also able to find friends and feel accepted. It was one of my best friends in high school that made it possible for me to attend my first game. I'll never forget it. It was an exciting time for me to attend my first Nebraska football game. However, I did get a ribbing from my friend and his dad because I wore blue to the game and we were playing Kansas that day. I was told that no matter what, you always had to wear red to a Nebraska game.

Since I was rarely ever shown love, I didn't know how to give it. It was a huge void in my life. I had a friend once make a statement that took me a long time to understand. She was rambling on about someone else, a friend or family member I don't know. But she finished the statement by saying, "They love me". She said it with such joy I thought she was being a geek. I could not imagine that someone could have the confidence to say such a thing.

My step-dad's philosophy on love and women could have been better. He taught me to tag them and bag them. Who was I to know better? In some ways, I wished he hadn't preached that. In others, I am glad he did. So, I can tell others not to live or think that way. Because of what he taught me women became more of a statistic than anything else.

Like I said before, how was I to know better I wasn't shown any love by my real parents. My father never showed my mom any love, nor did she do the same for him. He treated her like a punching bag for the most part. I never saw them kiss or hug each other nor did they ever say "I love you" to each other. They shared the same birthday and never celebrated it. I don't even know how they got together in the first place. They both had a cold demeanor, especially toward each other and the same could be said with my mom and step-dad. They never showed much affection to each other except after they had been drinking and that was only if they weren't fighting over something stupid.

When it came to women, I didn't treat them right because I didn't know-how. Sure, I had a few long- term relationships if you consider six months long term. But were they meaningful? "No". But I was only after one thing. I felt at times that what I was doing was right. That was the way to get girls to love me. But sex does not turn into love. Not once, did I ever have a relationship where that happened. It may have been strong feelings on my behalf but it was never love.

I can say with all honesty, that I did not treat them like my father treated my mom. I would romance them a little, but it wasn't to gain a lasting relationship. Then again, when you think about it, I was no different than my father. I did not physically abuse them but I did abuse them emotionally. I can testify and I will throughout this book. Emotional scarring is a lot deeper and more severe than anything physical. For all the women that I hurt, I would like to say I am sorry to every one of them. I can only hope that they have or will forgive me.

As I look back at those days. There were some girls that I think I truly loved and probably could have had a longer-term than six months with them. I have got to give them credit for reading between the lines and seeing that I had the right intentions but just didn't handle it properly. I wonder if and how my life would have turned out if I had only treated them differently.

After going to college for only one year, I moved in with my grandma for a couple of years off and on. During that time, I was working a couple of part-time jobs as well as pulling Army reserve duty one weekend every month. When I wasn't staying with my grandma, I would stay with friends. I partied like I always did. I never had a desire to stop. I thought I was having a good time. Then again, I was a young kid, probably no different than most. Exploring life and spreading my wings.

After a couple of years of being in the Army reserve, I decided to give active duty a try. I knew I needed something more in my life. I wasn't worried about going in. I had already had a taste of the Army life, plus I had a strong desire to travel. So, I felt the Army had something for me. Even though I was alone, I was used to it. Yet, I wasn't alone as there were several other guys just like me. Somehow that helps you build a strong camaraderie. I also felt that those same people were not judgmental. Other than sports, for the first time in my life, I felt accepted and appreciated.

The Army filled many voids that I had in my life. Mostly structure and discipline. I was always a good worker, just as I feel that I was always a good person. I felt I could be better if only I had the proper environment. One other thing the Army did for me is it eliminated all the drama that I was used to. I was surrounded by good people that were a part of something special. I learned how to respect authority which wasn't easy. After all, when I was younger I had a problem with this but it all depended on what type of authority. Coaches, yes, teachers, maybe and parents, depending on the circumstances. I learned more about authority as a leader than as a follower. I learned how important it was to get those following you motivated to accomplish the mission. Because of that, I feel that the times I was in charge made me more respectful of the times I wasn't.

While I was stationed at Fort Benning Georgia, I met
a guy who for a while was my closest friend. We did
everything together. In the spring of 1988, he had
fulfilled his time in service. During that same time, I had
received orders that I was on my way to Germany. As
you can imagine we had one massive party celebrating
our time together. What was nice was we stayed in
contact over the next three years. It was he that kept
sending me postcards of women in bikinis from Florida.
He attempted to get me to get out and come live with
him. It eventually worked. It was those same postcards
that I taped to my wall locker that Private Edwards saw
and got uncomfortable with.

As a child I had a dream of maybe becoming a police
officer. Because of that, I re-enlisted for the military
police in 1989 and got out in 1991. Being a military
policeman was nothing I had imagined. It downright
stunk. Because I was in combat arms before, my unit
thought it was best I trained the new troops instead of
doing any sort of real police work. When the time came
for me to re-enlist. I chose to get out. Not only that but I
knew the Army was downsizing. I thought to myself, I

was still young enough and in great shape and I have learned so much. It was time to take on the real world again. I contacted my buddy and asked him if the offer still stood. He said, "I was more than welcome". So, I moved to Florida. We were roommates for a couple of years and stayed friends for maybe a couple of more after that. Things didn't end up that way as we grew apart from each other and saw things differently.

The first thing I needed to do was get a job. I answered an ad from the paper which came from an employment agency. They helped me get a job with a fast-food restaurant as a manager trainee. I wasn't too sure if this is what I wanted to do. But, I found it easy as well as fun. Especially compared to what I had done in the military. The next thing you know I am getting promoted at a rapid pace and became a store manager in about eighteen months. It was a rewarding time for me. Again, just like the Army I was feeling accepted and appreciated. Above all, I felt like I was on top of the world.

It was through this job that I met my wife, she worked at the bank that handled our account. When I would go to get a change order or drop off the previous night's deposit, she would usually be the one who helped me. We began to talk more and more and became friends very quickly. I never pursued her because I noticed she had a wedding ring on. The friendship continued to the point where she would come to visit me during her lunch period. Then there would be times she would swing by the drive-thru after she got off work to get a soda or a dessert. This went on for a few months. I finally noticed she stopped wearing her wedding ring. I never made any inquiries into that, I just left it alone.

One day after work, I stopped by the bank to make a deposit. I could have easily gone to the night drop but wanted to go inside to see her. As I was walking up to the door, I met the security guard who I had befriended during this time. I went to him and said, "I have a question for you." Before I could ask him the question, he replied, "All I know is, that before you started coming here, every day she would bring her lunch to work". " Now she's going to see you for lunch". What surprised me was he knew the answer before I gave him the question. The chemistry between us must have been more obvious than I thought.

So, that is how my wife and I got started. My relationship with her was not like any other. I showed her respect, love, and kindness. I wasn't trying to make her a statistic like the others. I did not know what was specifically different about her, but she was definitely unique. I went on to romance her in so many ways, I treated her like a queen. In return, she was very good to me as well.

One night I helped her out by picking up her girls from the daycare. By then she had moved into a new house on her own. She had become legally separated from her husband. As I was taking the kids home, the youngest one asked me, "Are you going to be our new daddy?" I inquired, "Do you want me to be?" She said, "Yes, you're funny."   I felt very honored.

We had an awesome relationship that lasted roughly a year and a half when I had the notion to ask for her hand in marriage. It was quite obvious that I had the approval of the girls. I got along great with her family as well. I just knew she was the one. I felt so comfortable with all of this that I was able to get assistance from her family to help me with all the preparations for my proposal.

After I bought the ring, I gave it to her mother to keep for me. Her grandmother also helped me prepare to pop the question. We tied the ring to a silk rose with a red ribbon and we placed it in a box that we had to alter so that we could enclose it into yet another box. I was planning everything for Christmas day in front of her entire family.

On that particular Christmas morning, we spoiled each other with gifts. We spent the morning at her house opening presents and having a big breakfast. Later that day, we headed out to her parent's house to have Christmas dinner. Neither one of us knew that the other had more surprises in store for each other. I dressed up that day with a shirt and tie with nice slacks. She asked me why I was so dressed up. I replied, "I always get dressed up for Christmas." Yes, I told her a little white lie because I dressed that way for the proposal. After we got to her parent's home, she handed me more presents to open. She bombarded me with all sorts of Nebraska memorabilia. I was completely surprised and loved every moment of it.

The entire time we were there, I was getting more nervous by the minute. It showed because I was having more than the usual amount of beer. Then, just as dinner was ready, her mom (which was part of the plan) walked into the bedroom and carried out a big box and placed it at my wife's feet. As she got to the box with the ring, I knelt in front of her and asked her if she would marry me in front of her entire family. All the while her sister was recording the entire event. I guess you can say that I am glad she said "Yes". How embarrassing would that have been if she said "No".

We went on to have a wonderful relationship. She is truly an amazing woman. She is loved by everyone she meets. She has a heart of gold. She is always giving and very thoughtful towards others. In a sense, I have hit the jackpot. I can only hope and pray to be the kind of person she is.

A couple of months after we were engaged, my step-dad passed away. I went home for the funeral. While I was there, I started to realize how much I missed Nebraska. When I got back home, my fiancé and I discussed taking a vacation and going to Nebraska to visit. There is something about that state that tugs at my heartstrings. It is more than the football team. It is the food, the culture and overall a wonderful place to grow up. It is the great Midwestern values that people have, it is the heartland of America and I wanted to share all of that with her.

Shortly after our return from vacation to Nebraska, we discussed the possibility of moving there. She was all for it but, it had to be discussed with her ex-husband. After all, he was the girl's father and had visitation with them every other weekend. Not to forget the fact that he was very good at paying his child support. They had discussed the option of us moving, He told her he was alright with it. Sometime later I moved up there to get everything established. I found a job right away with a fast-food restaurant, naturally. I also started looking at new home models and possible school districts for the girls. I had everything going fairly well.

After being there for a few months my fiancé came up to visit and spent time interviewing with area banks for a job. Her interviews went so well that she pretty much had a choice of a couple of banks to work for.

Shortly after she returned to Florida, she was surprised to learn that her ex-husband filed a motion to stop her from taking the girls out of state. Apparently, he had a change of heart. To be honest with you I didn't blame him. I would have done the same thing. There was also the possibility that he was trying to ruin our relationship. When I told you that I finally went to jail for fighting, It was him that I got into a fight with.

My fiancé hired an attorney. He eventually contacted me in Nebraska. He told me that I was going to be vital to the case and that I needed to return for the trial. He also informed me that it was best that we got married before we went to court. He said that there would be no way a judge would keep a husband and wife separated.

So here we are, we had a little over a month to plan our wedding and prepare for court. I flew down on a Monday, we got married on Tuesday. We went to court on Wednesday, which of course took all day and I flew back out on Thursday. So, that is how I spent my wedding and if you want to call it, a honeymoon. We, in reality, spent our honeymoon evening going over all our notes for the hearing.

After the hearing, the judge said that there was so much for him to consider that he would need some time. A couple of weeks later I got a phone call from my wife. I could tell she was different. Since she didn't mention anything about the trial, I assumed she was just having a bad day. Finally, she broke down and gave me the news. The judge granted her everything in the case, except the move to Nebraska. We were both devastated. We spent the entire evening going over and making plans so I could move back to Florida.

My life in Florida was not as good as before. For whatever reason, I was unable to get work anywhere, even though I thought I had an outstanding resume. I was willing to do almost anything. The jobs I did get, did not pay well or the people were impossible to work for.

My wife noticed I was becoming more, irritable and cranky. I wasn't the same lovable person I once was. She proposed that I go back to Nebraska to get work which was pretty much guaranteed for me and in turn I would be happy. She told me that she loved me too much to see me suffer. She also suggests that we would try to take her ex-husband back to court again. Little did we know at the time, that the judge's decision was final. Just because we didn't like the outcome did not give us cause to retry. The only other option we had would be if she moved to Nebraska without the girls. With the notion of when the girls reached the age of thirteen, they could then decide who they wanted to live with. That meant it would be three years for the oldest and six for the youngest. She would never leave her girls, nor would I ask her too. As miserable as I was in Florida, she would be worse in Nebraska.

So here I am, I finally meet this wonderful woman with a wonderful and loving family. But in the middle of it all, I was feeling all alone again. Was I ever going to find true happiness? Was I ever going to meet that special someone who I could love and love me for the rest of my life? What about kids? Despite the question, the youngest girl asked me about being their father. The girls never once called me "Dad". I wanted children. I wanted a normal family. But maybe it wasn't meant to be.

I went back home to Nebraska and got my old job back. I rented an apartment and was doing well. My wife visited whenever she could; sometimes with the girls and others not. But as you could expect, something was missing. Outside of the obvious that we had a long distant relationship, I wasn't happy. Then there was the fact, even though I was married. I still wanted to go out. I was lonely and all alone again.

Two years had passed when we realized that the move for her and the girls was unrealistic. I sure was not going to move to Florida again. Even though we loved each other as much as we did, we talked about divorce. She did not have it in her heart to go through all the hassle with the lawyers and such so she asked me to handle the entire ordeal on my end, which I did. Our divorce became final in January of 2000.

That was the beginning of a long and treacherous time for me. I thought I knew what I wanted. But I didn't like what I got. I went back to my partying ways, dating a slew of girls. Before you know it, I was told that I was going to be a daddy from a woman I just started to date. I wanted kids, but not this way. I wanted a wife with those kids, a wife that I could have a strong relationship with, and one that I would grow old with. That wasn't happening. What had happened was my womanizing had come back to haunt me. I had heard rumors in the past that I may have been a father more than once. This time it was for real. I was only in this relationship for less than four months when I was told I was going to be a father. I felt I needed to stay in this relationship for the baby. I wished I hadn't because she caused me a lot of grief.   I thought I was in love, who was I to know better? I would have been better off just paying child support and having weekend visits with my kid.

Couples shouldn't have that much drama in the early stages of a relationship. But this one did. Why I decided to stay with this one is beyond me. Was it because I thought I was in love? Was it because I knew she had issues and thought I could help her? Was it because I felt I was getting too old to find someone else? Was I getting desperate? These were a few questions that ran through my head. Needless to say, I stayed with it.

The drama escalated to arguments. She had a trust issue, she thought I was cheating on her. I once heard that only the guilty accuse. I told her about that. Of course, she denied everything. The more I got to know her and learn of her past the more suspicious I got. I guess I should have paid attention to the signals I was getting. The rumors I heard about her were starting to come to light. I was seeing first-hand how she could get after drinking. She got quite flirty and didn't care who saw or what they said about it. Including me.

She did give up drinking once she found out she was pregnant. But what concerned me was she smoked more than before. I tried to encourage her to quit smoking. Her response was, "I will if you don't drink". I thought to myself "Man does she have some issues or what?" Now, these issues are mine because of the baby. Did I get in over my head?

I know that women can become very emotional when they are pregnant, but she took this to the extreme. She was bad before she got pregnant and got worse after. Sometimes I wonder if she didn't act out on purpose. Was this just part of her plan?

When I tried to teach her structure as well as how to manage her money better and instill in her that you have to work hard to get ahead in life. It seems like she was unwilling to adhere to what I was teaching her. I knew my childhood was rough. It sounded like hers could have been worse. If what she told me was true. She apparently was molested by her uncle. She used that as a crutch as to why she may have been promiscuous at times. I tried to help her through it all but I could only do so much. Some people just have a hard time with certain things in life.

I took her to a really nice upscale restaurant one evening for dinner. I can tell you in all honesty. She didn't know how to act. It was almost like she felt intimidated. Or that she wasn't used to nice things or someone treating her so well. I thought her behavior was kind of cute that night. Or as I reflect on it, could it have been an act?

As time progressed in the relationship, I realized I was being played. She asked me to teach her finances such as managing a checking account. So, I helped her. She did well with it. After we moved in together, we got a joint checking account as she realized how important it was to work as we needed a second income. She acted like she was trying to put her best foot forward. All of that came to a head very quickly. I found out as she was writing checks that never got deposited to the appropriate accounts. She would log entries in the bank journal, write out the check, and then destroy them. Take the money out and what she did with it is beyond me. The next thing I know is I am getting my 1995 Pontiac Firebird repossessed. The sad thing about it is that I had only nine payments left on a sixty-month note. Then came the disconnect notices and the eviction notice. Her little plan had caught up with her and unfortunately me as well.

One night in August of 1999 while she was away at work, I spent the evening with some friends at their home. They invited me over and asked me to bring my dog to play with their new puppy. We had a barbecue and a few beers. I finally got home around 10 pm. She showed up roughly half an hour later. She said she tried to call me all night and accused me of fooling around on her. I argued my case, but she wouldn't listen. Then we started fighting over the bills. I told her that I entrusted her with the checking account and paying the bills. She tried to deny everything even though I had no car and a handful of notices to include the eviction letter, which she was unaware of. (I took it off the front door and kept it hidden,

Knowing we would probably have this moment). She denied stealing from me and was trying to turn the entire situation around and put the blame on me.

We went to bed angry at each other. I thought it would be best if I crashed on the sofa in the basement. I figured she went to sleep in our bed. However, she was up all night planning her next move. Around 6 am the next morning, I was awakened by the police. They took me outside to place me next to their cruiser to ask me a few questions. They told me they were taking me in for domestic violence. I was still sleepy at that time but woke up quickly. She had told them that I beat her up. While one officer was questioning me, the other was taking pictures of the inside of her mouth. I asked the one officer, "If I hit her so hard to cause damage to the inside of her mouth, then why wasn't there a bruise on the outside?" He told me that was for the judge to decide. They also charged me with terrorist threats because I left her a voicemail and called her a name along the lines of a female dog. That charge later got dropped.

I was taken away to jail that morning. My bail was set at seven thousand dollars so I needed seven hundred dollars to get out. I was fortunate enough to get a friend to do all the legwork to get me bailed out. She got my check from my employer, brought it to me in jail so I could sign it over to her. She cashed it and then bailed me out. This would be the same friend that would bail me out a year later because of the same girlfriend. The same friend that was once a friend of hers as well, that later warned me of her. I got out by noon on that same day. I was told I could not go home, even though everything in the house was mine, more importantly, my dog was there. I was not leaving her behind for anything. My friend took me to my house as I sat in the car. She retrieved my dog and a few of my possessions. She informed me that it looked like my girlfriend had left. Once I found out she did, I could occupy my home again.

Later that week, I received a strange phone call from my girlfriend's friend who lived in Seattle, Washington. She was probing me for information as to my girlfriend's whereabouts. Little did I know my girlfriend was there all along. That explains where some of my money went. A couple of days later, he got up the nerve to talk to me on her own. She called me and the first thing she did was apologize for what she had done. She told me she wanted to come home and make everything right. To her credit, she tried, I think.

After she got back, she went to the prosecutor's office to get the charges dropped. They were somewhat to the degree that the domestic violence was dropped to a third-degree assault. I was told by my attorney that even if she did not want to press charges that the prosecutor's office could still file charges if they saw fit.

Because it was a crime of violence they were moving
forward with some sort of charge.

The court system made me meet with a pretrial
investigator. I felt like I was already on trial by some of
the questions he asked. I do not remember exactly
what I said because I was so nervous. All I knew was
that I was being judged unfairly and I didn't know how to
handle myself. This investigator had me feeling like I
was some sort of hardened criminal. They brought up
my previous arrest records since I had been jailed for
assault before I surely was guilty now. They went so far
as to bring up the DUI and minor in possession charges.
They said it was showing a pattern. I was stuck
between a rock and a hard place and had no way of
getting out of this one. I was done no matter what. What
got me, was why wasn't my attorney there with me
during the pretrial questioning?

My trial was in November of that year. My court-
appointed attorney used my girlfriend as a witness. The
prosecutor was not happy with that. Regardless, she
told the judge that she had lied and made the whole
thing up. The judge looked at her in shock. The

prosecutor objected to her comment and said something along the lines that this was a typical response from battered women. That they generally show remorse and do not want to cause their mates any harm. He further stated that I was a monster and deserved jail time. He went so far as to compare me to O.J. Simpson and said she could end up like his wife Nicole.

I was looking at a one-year jail sentence. Instead, I got four weekends of jail time and two years of probation. Somehow, I think the judge believed her when she spoke up. I think he put her comments into consideration when he sentenced me. I got that feeling when I noticed the prosecutor's reaction. He was not happy.   Like I said before I felt she tried to make things better. Her demeanor was better, sweeter, more caring, and giving.

She dropped me off on Friday nights to serve my weekend in jail. Then she picked me up on Sunday evenings. When we got home, she would tell me about all she has done around the apartment to make it look more like home. She cooked really nice meals for me

and made sure I had beer in the refrigerator. I thought
she was truly sorry. I was willing to forgive her.

We went on to have a decent relationship considering
what all had acquired. We had a real nice Christmas
and Valentine's Day. Then in April, our beautiful baby
girl was born. It was on a Wednesday, just past
lunchtime when I got a call from my supervisor that I
needed to go home because my girlfriend was about to
go into labor. When I got home I found her packed and
ready to go. I got her loaded up into the car and took
her to the hospital. We had been there for a while when
they decided that she was going to need an epidural to
help with the delivery. We waited and waited. So long
that I could no longer stay awake. Wouldn't you know it
around 2 am there was this tremendous scream? It was
my girlfriend and it was time. My little girl was on the
way to meet the world. She brought so much joy and
excitement to my life. I was truly a proud father, I took
her everywhere I went and showed her off to everyone I
knew.

When I got to hold her for the first time, my heart
couldn't stop pounding. I was so excited to be a father.

She was so beautiful. She took my heart from the first second I laid eyes on her. I was so excited that I almost passed out. It was a good thing that I was no longer holding her at the time. The nurses made me sit down and forced me to drink some water.

It was six a.m. and I couldn't go to sleep from all the excitement. The nurses assured me that everything was alright and that I should go and get some rest. They said that mom and baby would need some rest as well. So, I went home. I wasn't too sure if I was in any condition to drive from the lack of sleep, but I made it. When I got home, I decided to take a shower. Once I got in it, I felt compelled to get on my knees and thank God, for such a beautiful child. I cried, prayed, and thanked him like none other. Afterward, while I was getting dressed. I thought maybe I can do this God thing. I am going to go back in time here. I had said earlier that I had met a man while at the gym who invited me to his church. This had been around the first of the ear. Three months before my daughter was born. Now here I am praying to God, who I did not know.

A couple of days later the two got to come home. Everything was wonderful but that would only last for a couple of months. By the time July came around, everything went south very fast. My girlfriend and I had taken our daughter to a friend's house to celebrate the Fourth of July. He lived thirty miles outside of Omaha. I thought it would be nice to get out to the country and have a nice evening. I thought we were going to have a nice time. But we didn't. She started to act strangely that night. At first, I thought it was because she had a tendency to be shy.   But I could sense something was wrong. This would end up being the last time we did anything together.

Later that week, I started a part-time job working evenings as a delivery person for restaurants that offered take out food. Even though I had a full-time construction job, I needed to make up the money lost from the incidents earlier in our relationship. Since I no longer had my Firebird. We had to purchase a used car that we had to have put in her name. This was the car that I was going to use for the delivery position.

After my first night of work, I went home to discover the locks at the apartment had been changed. I went to ask my next-door neighbor if he knew what was going on. He told me that my girlfriend had the maintenance crew switch out the locks. He also said he overheard her tell the maintenance man that she had filed a police report telling them I stole her car. "Here we go again!" I said to myself.   So I borrowed a screwdriver and hammer from him. From there I broke the door open, grabbed my dog, and some personal items and left.

This time I was ready for her. I wasn't too sure what she was up to. But I knew it was not good. I went to spend the night at a friend's house. I got up extra early the next morning and went back to the apartment. I parked where she couldn't see the car so I wouldn't give myself away. I went up to the apartment, sat, and waited for her. I brought my dog along for two reasons. One for protection and the other thinking that my girlfriend wouldn't do anything that would cause her any harm or discomfort. After what happened I wish for the life of me I hadn't brought her.

She eventually showed up with a girlfriend of hers and our daughter. She had no idea I was there. I could see and hear them outside the apartment as the parking lot was right outside our windows. I went to hide in the bedroom. Just waiting for that right moment to come out. When I did, I startled her, which was surprising because I was sure I would have given myself away considering what damage I did to the door the night before. The look on her face was priceless. I bet she thought I was in jail or somewhere else, anywhere but back at the apartment.

I asked her what she was up to this time. She couldn't or wouldn't say a thing. Her girlfriend looked scared out of her mind. Probably asking herself, "What in the world did I get myself into"? She and her girlfriend ended up leaving. Because she had my daughter with her, I know she wasn't prepared for whatever plan of action she thought she might have. After they left, I grabbed my dog and went back to the car. Along the way, I was trying to figure out what she was up to as well as what my next move would be. I figured I was going to have to beat her at her own game. Then my evil plan started to take shape. After she came back from Seattle when she was trying to correct all the wrong she had done. She admitted to me that she bit the inside of her mouth to make it look as if I had harmed her. It finally hit me because she had a nervous twitch about her where she would do that on occasion. To beat her at her own game, I decided to punch myself in the eye. I know that was wrong. But I felt my back was up against the wall. Besides, I was used to it. After all, I used to punch myself in the face before a fight.

I pulled into a gas station and used the payphone to call the police. I told them that she had hit me. They said they were sending out a unit to take my report. This next part I don't understand because some how they were able to reach her. Because just a few minutes after the police showed up, so did she. This was pre-cell phone days where not everybody had one. Shortly after that, there was a second officer that showed up on the scene.

After the officers conversed with each of us and then with each other. They arrested me for stealing the car and trespassing. Then there was this huge surprise on her face. She thought she was only there to retrieve her car but they arrested her too. I only wish I could have read her mind at that time. The sad thing was our daughter was taken by her girlfriend, and my dog was taken to the humane society.

They took both of us to jail. Wow, here we go again. Since this was a Saturday afternoon, we were placed in holding cells and would be there until Monday morning to see the judge. Surprisingly we were in neighboring cells. I guess there wasn't much segregation there as far as male form female. She tried desperately to talk to me and tell me she was sorry again and that she loved me. I told her I wasn't buying any of it this time. I didn't care what she had to say.

Here comes Monday morning, off to see the judge. We were in the same courtroom to see the same judge. The only different thing was her charges were dropped and she walked out. I, on the other hand, was being held with a bond of $3,000. The only thought that went through my mind at that time was, "How did she beat me again?" I mean seriously what was she saying to people about me? What was she doing?

It took me a week to get out, mostly due to the fact both my ex-wife and probation officer were on vacation that week. Talk about bad timing. When I did, the first thing I did was retrieve my dog from the humane society. The poor thing did not eat all week and was hoarse from all the barking. She was a feisty old girl and I can just bet she gave the folks at the humane society a hard time.

Here I am again being charged for a crime I did not commit. What is worse this time was, I was on probation from the previous time. Thankfully I was able to get the charges dropped all due to my probation officer. The two of us had several talks about the health of the relationship between my girlfriend and me. He never directly said it, but he was trying to tell me to get away from her. She was nothing but trouble and not good for me. He could see right through her. He knew that we only had the one car. He also knew I was starting a second job. He most definitely knew where I lived. That was his argument, how could I be charged with trespassing in my own home? After all, I was the primary name on the lease.

The apartment complex tried to get me to pay for the damages done to the door. I eventually ended up winning that situation quite easily. I helped them realize that they had allowed the maintenance crew to change locks on my apartment without my permission. When they realized they were at fault, they backed off. They did tell me they were not going to honor the remainder of my lease and that I needed to move out as quickly as possible. I responded by telling them I would move when I was good and ready. Besides the way they acted, I didn't want to stay there any longer anyway. I further stated that they did not have much authority in the situation. That all of this came about because of their negligence. I also told them that if they wanted any money for the damages, to go after my ex-girlfriend. As time went on I realized I wasn't going to get my deposit back and decided I wasn't going to pay rent any further. Good thing for them that I moved out in about forty-five days.

What it comes down to is this. When I was looking for love, I never received it. When I did get it I didn't know how to handle it, and when I thought I had it, I sure didn't want it.

Chapter 5

Rebirth

I couldn't believe that I had been suckered twice by the same person. How does that saying go? "Fool me once, shame on you, fool me twice, shame on me". Because I couldn't reach my probation officer. I reached out to the same friend who had previously helped me get bailed out, but she did not have the money. Since I had no access to my money. All I could do was wait until I could get a hold of my ex-wife or probation officer. My last paycheck was stolen from my girlfriend. What was sad about that was I tried to press charges on her for that. It went nowhere. How does that happen? I got a copy of the check once it cleared. I showed the police where she forged my signature on the back of it and was able to cash it. I was told there was nothing they could do. Seriously, how was she doing all of this? I finally reached my ex-wife on Friday night, thankfully, she was able to help me. She got a hold of my friend, wired the money to her so she could get me out of jail.

That week was rough for me. Since I did not know
exactly what was going to happen to me, my mind went
crazy. Here I am on probation, again facing charges of
a crime I did not commit. I was deeply depressed to the
point I wanted to commit suicide. All I could think about
was ending it all. Because of my mindset they put me in
a special cell here I could not hurt myself. They had a
camera on me the entire time. As I sat in my cell, I got
mad and started screaming at God. I was blaming him
for all my troubles. I yelled at him and blamed Him for
all the injustices in my life. I faulted Him for giving me
such a beautiful daughter and then taking her away from
me. I was hating Him for all that was wrong. I even went
so far as to challenge His might. I told Him if He was so
powerful, to go ahead and end my life.

One night when I was having one of my tirades, the
nurse who was monitoring me could see the fit that I
was having. She asked me to speak to her through the
intercom system. Through our conversation, she was
able to calm me down quite a bit. She further went on to
invite me into her secured office so we could talk face to
face. I think she felt safe with me because if I was in her
shoes I am not sure if I would do such a thing. She

reached out to me with such a kind and gentle spirit. She was truly an Angel. She was so loving and caring about my disposition. She went so far as to offer me some homemade cookies that she had brought in that night. I think that was the only thing I had to eat all day. Due to my frame of mind, food was the last thing I wanted.

We sat and talked about God, she talked, I just listened. She said so many wonderful things to me that night about Him. She promised me that He loves me no matter what, that He was truly an awesome God and that He would take care of my problems as long as I learned to trust Him. She was so detrimental in aiding me from doing anything stupid to myself. I wish I knew her name so I could call her up and thank her from the bottom of my heart. I think she would be very pleased to see how I have turned out. Because she treated me the way she did. The thought of suicide seemed stupid. With that my confidence started to return and all I knew was that no matter what, I had to make things right again.

After I got out of jail, I started to make plans on what I needed to do next. I made a few phone calls. One of them was to my mom. She informed me that my ex-girlfriend had been in touch with her and that she wanted to talk to me. I was very skeptical because I could no longer trust her. The only thing that kept going through my mind was that old cliché, but I wanted to see my daughter. I was scared for her and her future. I did not want her childhood to turn out like mine.

Something else crossed my mind which was scary. I once heard people tend to want to be with someone like their parents. For instance, a woman may want to marry someone like her father. A father who gave her love and a sense of security. A man may want to marry someone like his mother, someone who is loving and nurturing. Well, my ex-girlfriend as I was discovering was an awful like my mom. I could trust neither one of them.

I realized that the two of them were similar and I didn't want to marry anyone like my mom. I figured I needed to buck this trend. I wanted nothing to do with her and I sure was not going to trust anything she said.

Both of these women did things to others for no reason despite how much that person may have cared for them. These two were not to be trusted. I couldn't figure out for the life of me why they could not handle stability or normalcy in their lives.

After giving it much thought, I eventually gave in and agreed to meet with my ex. Most of this was due to my daughter. We began to see each other every two to three days. When we did it was only for a moment at a time and in a public place with a lot of people around. In the first few visits, she didn't bring my daughter. Because of that, I was very cautious with every move I made around her. I was always looking over my shoulder to see if there may be a police officer coming up to arrest me for who knows what else. I was in a serious state of paranoia. During our visits, she wanted to talk about things that weren't of any significance to me. Every topic she brought up, I switched gears and asked about my daughter. Because of that she eventually started to bring her so I could see her.

One night she asked if she could come over to the apartment and offered to bring my daughter. Who was I to say "No"? I wanted to see my little girl. She went so far as to promise me everything would be fine. So, I allowed it against my better judgment. To my surprise, we ended up having a very nice evening. We had dinner, watched a movie, and had a relaxing evening. It seemed to me as she was trying to make amends for everything. However, I had been down this road before. I was not letting my guard down. I figured as long as she was on my turf, I had the upper hand. She ended up staying the night. The next morning, I got up to go to work, with that I said my goodbyes and kissed my daughter.

That night when I returned home from work, they were gone, gone for good. I wish I could say I was surprised but nothing about her surprised me anymore. She took all of her belongings which was not much except for a cedar chest her grandmother supposedly gave her. Which I thought was weird because it had such sentimental value to her. Her grandmother who had raised her, passed away a month before our daughter was born. Though she wanted to go to the funeral she didn't. Her doctor advised her to not make such a long and emotional trip that close to her due date; He said the stress may cause her to go into premature labor. Later on, some female friends of mine would tell me she left the chest for a reason. She would use that as an excuse to come back. That never happened.

As time went by I tried to find her. Not necessarily for her, but more for my daughter. My searches came to dead ends. I couldn't give up on my daughter regardless of what kind of person her mother was. She had taken my little girl; my pride and joy. Even though I had that talk with the nurse in jail, a lot of those old feelings were starting to resurface. I wasn't thinking about suicide, how could I. But a state of depression was starting to set in again.

My searches led me to her ex-husband. He was no fan of hers either. He told me that she moved out of state. He thought she had moved back to her home in Missouri but wasn't sure. He didn't care as he informed me that she had filed a motion in the courts to have her parental rights removed. He wanted to break all ties with her no matter what and do what was right for his kids. It was then when I realized I was dealing with someone who had more problems than I could handle. Through her ex-husband, she had three children and one other child from a guy before she met me. She gave up on all four children. She turned her back on them.

What kind of mother would do such a thing? What bothered me more was why did she keep my child? Why was she torturing not just me but my daughter like this?

I went back to doing what I thought I did best. I started drinking again every night. My daughter was gone and I couldn't find her. My life was completely ruined. Depression had set in and I saw no light at the end of the tunnel. I decided I had a new best friend and his name was Jim Beam. I was putting down almost a bottle every night. It was cheap and effective. After all, I wasn't paying my bills anymore. What else would I spend my money on?

I knew I needed a change so I left the apartment and moved in with a friend of mine for a short while. The only problem with living with him as everyone else who knew him lived there too. It was a constant party every night. Though I was drinking myself, I didn't need that environment, I needed solitude. I needed my drinks, but I also needed to be alone to figure out what I needed to do next. By the end of October, I answered an ad for a live-in roommate. The guy who laced the ad was nice. As well as was his roommate. They were both in their late fifties or early sixties. When I first met them, I got a kick out of them. All they kept saying was "Around here, we drink beer". It sounded good to me.

I rented the basement for three hundred dollars a month with all utilities paid. It was a pretty good deal for a guy who was struggling financially and needed to get back on his feet. It was pretty much like an apartment. I had my own private access as well as a bathroom, a small fridge, and microwave. What more did I need?

I was still working my construction job which was nice because most of the job sites were close to my new home. Since my car had been repossessed, I ended up going through a buy here, pay here car lot and become the proud owner of a 1988 Chevy Beretta with close to two hundred thousand miles on it. But it ran and got me

129

where I needed to go. I had fallen on hard times. I came from an era in which I had the credit to own a brand- new car and close to buying a home, to now this.

Even though my new roommates drank a lot they were pretty mellow guys. They didn't throw parties nor did they encourage me to drink as my desire to drink started to wane. Don't get me wrong I still did, ust not every day. I did, however, drink more during Nebraska football games. My roommates were also pretty good about leaving me alone. So, I stayed to myself down in the basement, just me and my good ole' dog.

For those of you that are pet owners, you can truly understand how much comfort it was for me to have my dog during those tough times. No matter my mood or how heavy my heart, she always greeted me at the door ready to love me. I think all along she was telling me everything was going to be alright.

I spent many nights sitting in that basement, doing nothing more than soul searching. Because of that, I became an outcast from society.   While doing so, some questions or thoughts kept popping into my head.

Things like, Why, was this happening to me? Had my life of fighting and drinking taken me to this point? If people could see me now, I would be a laughing stock. Did I have a drinking problem? Why were things different from the days when I was married? What was next for me in my life? I was thirty-five years old, two years ago, I had it all going for me. I had a good job. Well respected, I had a new car, renting a house with an option to buy. Now here I am. Where was God? Was this all there was to my life? What was my purpose for existence? Then it hit me. Had I become the same as Private Edwards, the soldier I knew while I was in Germany? Thank God for that nurse that nurtured me while I was in jail. If I hadn't met her who knows where I would have ended up.

The truth be known is that God was there all along. He was trying to get my attention. He was saying to me, "Young man, have you had enough of this yet?" My soul searching and solitude state had me thinking so many things. It was this time where I reached deep down inside and said to myself "I have had enough I am going to get back on top no matter what".

My desire to ask God what was wrong with my life was becoming more evident. I was taking my first steps into Christianity. I was given a Bible by a friend and I found myself reading it every night. I would take it to work, sit in my car, and read it during lunch. When I didn't read it, I would just listen to the evangelists on the radio. Michael Youssef was who listened to the most. I carried this on at night as well except then I was watching TBN. I was doing everything to learn about God, his purpose for my life, and what was wrong with me. I had become engulfed in God.

I was praying every night on several topics. I even prayed throughout the day. Despite my feelings, I prayed for the return of my daughter and ex-girlfriend. I prayed for forgiveness, more understanding of the Bible, knowledge, and wisdom. You name it, I was praying about it. There were times I would pray for hours at a time. Prayer had become the only priority in my life.

However, I did not fully understand God one hundred percent. I was told by a dear friend of mine that I needed to put God first in my life and be sincere and honest for Him to fulfill the desires of my heart. It took me a long time to understand what she meant. I will get to that later. At that time my prayers were all about me and what God could do for me. I didn't quite understand salvation and how God was to save me. But I wanted to learn more.

During this period, I realized that maybe I should start attending church. The first church I attempted to go to was a church that my ex-girlfriend had ties to. Her sister knew the pastor there. I think I decided on that church so I could somehow feel attached to my ex. I went there on a Sunday night as opposed to Sunday morning. I don't know exactly why except to think I was probably drinking the night before. Anyway, they had a message on their marquee stating they held services at 6 pm. So, I decided to go. When I got there, I found it completely locked up. Not a sign of life anywhere. I couldn't believe it. "I was willing to give God a chance and he was turning his back on me is all I kept saying to myself. Then I started questioning if God was willing to accept me at all. After all, I never prayed to him or accepted him when I was younger. Instead, I mocked him. I was a womanizing drunk who beat people up. Maybe I didn't deserve his love and good graces. Then before I knew

it, I broke down and cried like I never had before. I cried
so much that I shouldn't have been driving. I was so
upset that when I got home, I did what I normally did, I
drank.

Weeks later I did go back to the church. Doing so, I
found out that they did meet that night. They planned
an event away from the church that was some sort of
fundraiser. Though I went on to attend a couple more
services there, something didn't seem right. So, I called
my oldest sister to ask her what I should do. She gave
me some advice on what type of church I should look
into. Luckily for me, there was one located only six or
seven blocks from where I lived. The previous church
was on the other side of town. As I look back at it, God
was directing me.

I started attending this new church regularly. My first
time was on a Wednesday night, which was Bible Study.
The people there were wonderful, they made me feel
welcomed. You could tell it was sincere. The pastor
was very kind as well. We ended up building a strong
relationship. On my days off, I liked to swing by his
office and just visit with him. He was a football fan like

me. It was refreshing to know that I could have a life with Christ and not give up my love for sports. The pastor showed interest in my spiritual growth. He was truly concerned that if I didn't make it for service on Sunday, I got a call that afternoon from him. He would call to see if everything was alright. I think he knew that I drank too. One Sunday afternoon, the day after a Nebraska game, he called me and asked if I had a hangover from the game and couldn't make it to church. After I hung up with him, I chuckled and said, "Man, you can't get anything past God!"

A few months after attending this church they announced they were going to have a baptismal ceremony. They were inviting all to partake if they have not done so prior. Of course, before you can partake in this ceremony you have to accept Jesus Christ into your heart as your Lord and Savior. I had already done this sort of in a way without the ritual of the church acknowledging it. This event occurred one wonderful evening when I saw the image of Jesus in my room. So, I decided to get baptized. There was me and one other lady who gave themselves to the Lord that night. It was such a wonderful evening. I invited my boss, his wife, and their two boys to attend. It made it an extra special evening to have someone there to share this with. I know that the Holy Spirit was with me and in me that night. I broke down and cried like none other that night. It was the Holy Spirit cleansing my soul as I surrendered myself to God.

Now let me describe that evening to you when I saw Jesus. One Thursday night in mid-October my routine had been almost like any other night. The only difference was that I was up later than normal. I had to get up at five-thirty to get to work by seven. As I was usually asleep by eleven.   I had read the Bible, said my prayers, and was lying in bed watching TBN. I can't remember for sure if it was the 700 club or not. But Gary Busey was a guest on this particular show. He was discussing his re-birth in Christ and how he got caught up in the wild party life in Hollywood. How the drugs and alcohol had overtaken his life. Finally, he talked about how he had been involved in a bad accident and was close to dying in the hospital. Then he made a commitment to God. He realized how precious his life was and that he was heading down the wrong path.

He also brought up some acronyms that I found quite interesting. He thought of these as he was lying in his hospital bed. Acronyms like the B.I.B.L.E. Basic Instructions Before Leaving Earth. As well as F.E.A.R. False Evidence Appearing Real . He also added F.A.I.T.H. and H.O.PE. Fantastic Adventures In Trusting Him and Heavenly Offerings Prevailing Eternally

For some reason the entire testimony he gave affected me in such a way that my heart started racing. I sat up and this sensation started rushing throughout my entire body. It was so wonderful that I didn't want it to end. I laid down to soak it all in and as I looked up towards the ceiling, I saw an image of Jesus looking at me. His arms were outstretched as if he was welcoming me into them. There was this feeling of peace and comfort. Yet, I was scared and excited all at the same time. I closed my eyes to see if they were playing a trick on me. They weren't. I started crying and thanking Jesus for coming into my life. I looked away for a moment and when I turned back, he was gone. The

sensation was still there though. I became so excited
that I couldn't go to sleep.

It was roughly an hour or two later when I prayed to
God, thanking him for this wonderful event, and asked
him to put me to sleep as I had to get up and go to work
the next morning. Before I knew it, I was out. Having
only a couple of hours of sleep, I couldn't believe how
rested I felt. I was rejuvenated like never before. I
would never be the same from that point on. I will never
forget that night. The only problem I would have was
that I didn't remind myself of that event every day. I'll
get to that later.

A Sunday or two after my baptism, there was this
elderly couple that asked me to sit next to them during
service. He was a retired pastor and I think she worked
for the school system. They made it a weekly routine
that my friend and I, the one who got baptized with me,
sit with them every Sunday. They were kind, sweet,
funny, and always cracking jokes. Their warmth and
good nature were exactly what I needed at that time as I
was starting my new life with God.

I attended that church for almost three years. During that time I had taken on a new career, got promoted, and had to move out of town. I was broken-hearted because I was leaving behind a really good church. I had made some good friends there. I tried to make it back a couple of times. It was just too long of a drive, especially during the winter months. I will never forget that church or the people. It was very instrumental in the beginning stages of my new-found faith.

My church in Lincoln had a large congregation. So big that they had three services every Sunday. I generally went to the second service. Because it was so big I found it hard to mingle with as many people as I did at my old church in Omaha   I did not know the senior pastor that well. The associate pastor generally greeted me every Sunday, when he did it was as if it was for the first time. I always got a kick out of that because it seemed that he didn't remember me from the week before. Eventually, I did manage to meet a few people which was nice as they were in the church softball teams. There was a league of nothing but church teams. What I liked about it was they had prayer before every game. Not only that, but it was also nice for me to get out and go play ball.

This church also had a constant schedule of Bible studies. I went to a few of them and I enjoyed them dearly. It still wasn't like home, I missed it when the pastor noticed that I wasn't in service and would call me. As well I missed the times when we could just sit in his office and talk about life or sports, that was nice. I did make it a point to call from time to time just to let him know how I was doing. Don't get me wrong, the church in Lincoln wasn't a bad church. I guess nothing will compare to the church where you got your start. Not only that, but I prefer a smaller community where everyone knew each other better.

My spiritual life in Lincoln had its ups and downs much like when I was in Omaha. My walk with the Lord had lost its luster after a year or two. It is nobody's fault but my own. I was still going to church on Sundays. I needed that to get me through the week, but I wasn't reading my Bible daily anymore. I was still drinking, but nowhere near what I used to do. To be honest with you I was unsure of what I could do or not do as far as a Christian was concerned. I figured I could still drink as long as I didn't act like a fool. I avoided fighting at all costs, except for one time. If only I could remember every day all day long the experience I had that night when I saw Jesus maybe my life would be much easier, but I didn't.

It didn't help that I went through a series of bad roommates. In one year, I had three roommates. One was a woman with her son who I could not figure out what her problem was. The second wanted to party too much. The third hit his girlfriend, and then took a shot at me when I stood up for her. After that, I was done with roommates. They were not helping me with my spiritual growth. I'm not blaming them; I just know they didn't help my cause. I found it best to get an apartment and live on my own.

As I said, I had lost my luster, the fire was burning out. But why? I had to realize that because I was a born again Christian, I was a child of Christ. Not just a child but a baby. Like all babies, you have to learn to crawl before you can walk and then run. You also have to eat baby food, before you can have solids. Just like the word of the Bible is food for your soul I was not feeding myself every day, I was no longer growing as a Christian.

I had some learning to do. I had to understand that even though God loves us unconditionally, I was not returning the same sort of love. I wasn't putting God first in everything I did. It took me a while to understand that. I had to discipline myself to stop living the life I was used to for the previous thirty-five or so years. I had to learn that there were false prophets out there. People who I thought possessed more knowledge on the Bible than me when in reality they didn't. These sorts of people would have me believing things that were not of God's word. I am not sure if they were trying to intentionally hurt me or not. As I experienced more of this. I realized it was the devil working through them to keep me away from God.

That is how the devil operates. He was after me like there was no tomorrow, by planting bad seeds in my life. He was successful to a degree. So much, that there became a time when I fell away from everything I had learned. Could it have been that I got oo comfortable or cocky with my spiritual life? That I felt that I could let my guard down. Could it have been that I had to go through this to appreciate what I had right after I got saved? I had lived all my life without God. I finally accepted him, saw his love, kindness, and good graces, and took it all for granted. Because of that, I slipped back into my old habits. Things were not going as well for me again. I tasted the good life and decided I wanted it back.

What I was becoming was a convenient Christian. I was manipulating what I knew about the Bible and using it to my benefit. I did not mean to do this. Just like most people, it was my sin nature that was taking over. It was the greed I had in my life. I had lost the understanding of how to put God first into my life.

With all of this, I noticed my temper was flaring up more frequently. This was the hardest of all my battles. Whenever I felt the desire to cuss someone out, I did. I made gestures to those who cut me off in traffic. I yelled at those when I ever felt wronged. I still punched things or tossed things around. I had forgotten how to control my anger by avoiding the word of God.

My anger issues kept taking me back to my youth.
Because I didn't have a good father figure in my
younger years. I became upset over that and was
feeling cheated in life. I was asking God why he had led
me down this road. For what purpose was I not afforded
a normal childhood. I wasn't asked to be brought into
this world. If I had, I surely wouldn't have asked for the
life that was given to me. It took me a while to learn
this, but by doing so it set me up to have a wonderful
relationship with God. He takes these circumstances
and turns them around into things of beauty.

After all of the misfortunes that I had been dealt with,
I became very untrusting of others.   I didn't know how to
trust and who to trust, which included God. I had been
thrown in jail twice for crimes I did not commit. Did I
deserve it after all the times I did hurt someone and had
not paid the price? Maybe so. I also got very defensive
if someone accused me of any wrongdoing.

There was a time when I felt all of this was coming
around again after I had taken on my new job. I was
one of two assistant managers at a retail store. We got
along, for the most part, considering his beliefs were not

the same as mine as a new Christian. But that didn't matter. There was also a third guy who was not a manager. He used to be during his previous employment with the company but he had to work his way back up again. After he was rehired, this third guy was jealous of the other assistant manager. To the point where he made comments to me periodically on how he didn't like this guy and that he was going to make him go away.

Sometime later, there was money missing from the store safe. It was first reported to be about five hundred dollars. It ended up being only three hundred.
Everyone in the store was told they would have an amnesty period to return the money and no questions would be asked. Unfortunately, that never happened.

The next step came in the form of all of us taking polygraph tests. The other assistant manager and I were the first on the list. Rumor had it that he and I were
being looked at because we both were hurting financially and we had access to the money. That didn't matter. All I kept thinking about was being thrown in jail

again for something I didn't do. That made me very nervous.

Then, I got a break. One night after a company softball game, the three of us, as well as a group of others, went to a bar to have a few beers. We stayed for a while and once the other assistant left, the third guy opened up his mouth on how he was getting his big break to be promoted. The alcohol was getting to him where he was getting loose lips. He made comments that pretty much implicated himself as the person setting this guy up. I made a couple of remarks in defense of this manager. He went on to accuse me of taking the money as if I were an accomplice. Like he was setting me up as well. He said he noticed how nervous I got whenever the discussion came up. I then realized when I had my time with the paleographer; I was going to have to bring this guy down. I was not going to allow him to frame me as well as the other assistant manager.

The time finally came. When I arrived at the polygrapher's office, I had a boost of confidence even though I was going to be hooked up to a machine that I wasn't sure I could trust. I sat through the instructions of

what was going to take place. I was told if I knew of
anything then I should speak up afterward. Right then
and there, I felt as comfortable as I could under the
circumstances.

After my test was completed, I was told that I had
passed with a 99.7% probability that I was telling the
truth. Then I got to tell my story. I told of all the
comments that this guy made. That he was setting up
the other manager and possibly me. The comments
had some validity to them. Enough that the
paleographer sat up and took notice. He then thanked
me for everything and dismissed me. The other
assistant manager was waiting n the lobby for his turn. I
was told not to say anything to him at all. I did,
however, sneak in a smile and a wink as if to tell him all
was going to be okay.

The next day the third guy was scheduled to go to the
polygrapher's office later in the afternoon to get tested
as well. He never made it that far. The company
learned of my statement and they changed the
schedule. They told the third guy he was going to be
going in that morning instead. He refused to go. He

was forced to have a meeting behind closed doors with the owner and the district manager. The next thing I know he and his buddy were going to their cars. When they returned, they both were carrying merchandise that belonged to the company…the merchandise they had stolen as well as a confession to the money.

I stated earlier that I could not trust anyone, not even God. But because of my circumstances, I realized that I had no choice in this matter but to trust God. It was the first time I felt I had to let everything go and let him handle it all for me. I was nowhere near the Christian I am today but I had to come to the fact that this time He was in my corner and He had to allow these things to happen for me to see how He was working in my favor.

The company I worked for had a collection department. I was aiding one of my employees in a collection matter. Through this, we had to leave notes on this customer's door. The customer and I didn't care for each other at all. After I had left a few enveloped notes at his place for a few days. He decided to take the envelopes and covered them with a powdery substance as well as he wrote the word "anthrax" on them. He called the police and reported that it was I, that did this. Since I was very active in trying to collect from this guy, he had my cell phone number saved on his phone.

One night after midnight I received a call from the police department. They asked me if they could send a unit out to talk to me. I agreed to it as well as I told them where I lived. They showed up in no time and took me into custody. Once I got into the interrogation room, I realized that I needed God right then and there.

During the interview process, I remained calm as I could though I was scared like crazy on the inside. I told the detective what I knew about this customer as well as what I knew about the relationship he and his girlfriend had. Once I got to tell my story, they knew I was telling the truth and took me back home.

Through his girlfriend, I found out that he was charged for falsifying a report among other things. She thanked me for all I did. I felt she was looking for a way to get out of this relationship and this was affording her the opportunity.

After all this, I learned how God works in all areas of my life. It probably would have been easier if my life wasn't poisoned with so much negativity. But, I learned that God can take bad situations and turn them into something good. I could write another book just from all my experiences on that topic alone.

One of the biggest things that separated me from God was the inability to forgive. I had so much anger and resentment and I found it very hard to forgive others. I also had to learn to forgive myself. If I made a mistake, I had to stop beating myself up over it. God accepted me when I was a sinner and I did not know Him. I had to understand that He would continue to accept me. God works in so many wonderful ways and I have never known of any two ways to be alike. That is what makes Him so great, that, and many others.

He used my love of sports to help me with my walk in life with Him. For instance, the Nebraska football team going through a rough couple of years taught me that there is more to life than football. That I was worshiping them more than Him and that was wrong. I learned there will be difficult times in life and He will see me through them as long as I trust in Him.

He used a story that I saw on television about a great basketball player to do work in me. It was when I was going through some difficult times with my Christianity. I saw this story about Larry Bird. It told how he was disciplined in his day-to-day preparations during the basketball season. Early on in his career he would go to the arena before most of the other players and practice his free throws. His free throw percentage was either the best in the league or close to it every season. He got comfortable with his performance and after a while, he stopped spending as much time with his pre-game warm-ups. His numbers started to falter. He realized he had to do what he was doing before and that was getting back to the basics.

Somehow God and his infinite ways got that message to me that I needed to do the same. I had to get back to the basics with my Christian lifestyle. Not just doing the everyday things such as reading the Bible, praying, and going to church. It was discipline in everything I did. I had to change my life in almost every aspect.

You can look at your Christian life like going on a diet. First of all, why are you on this diet? Could it be that you need a change in your life? When you go on the diet, you're being told that you can't eat certain foods. You also have to monitor how much you eat. When you start you notice things are different. You have to eat smaller portions, you cannot have desserts and you need to exercise. It's really difficult! You have to discipline yourself. You may need to have the encouragement and support of others.

Then all it takes is that one time where you either take that extra portion or decide to have that snack. Once you give in to temptation, you either feel guilty and don't do it again. Or, you say it was good and continue the bad habits which bring you back to square one. That is how temptation works in your life. Just a little doesn't seem to hurt though you know you shouldn't. Before you know it you are falling away from your goal and your heart's desire.

That is why it is so vitally important to put God first in everything you do. You have to ask yourself if He would be pleased with how you conduct yourself throughout the day. Are you cussing? Did you need to drink that beer? Could you have been nicer to that person on the road who cut you off? Could you have handled that indifference with he clerk without making a scene? Did you open the door for that older citizen at the store? You have to act as if God is right next to you because He truly is.

I have been on both sides and there is nothing better than being on the side of God. I have never had so much peace and love in my heart as I do now. The things that used to bother me no longer do and I find myself more tolerant of others. If you decide to have a relationship with God, it will be helpful to know this as well as many other things that I will discuss in the next few chapters.

One thing you need to probably know is that if God can change me and utilize me to help others then He can do the same thing with you. Do not be discouraged and do not give up.

Chapter 6

Getting Started

In this chapter I will discuss some of the basics of Christianity and why they are so important to know. Topics like sin, worshiping, and praying. As well as why it is so important to read the Bible every day. I will give general knowledge and words of encouragement.   I will also discuss the obstacles and roller coaster ride that you may encounter. Now you have to understand that I am not an ordained minister. I am just an "Average Joe". But because I have dealt with so much turmoil in my life and have lived on both sides of the fence. I feel my experiences will help you with your transition.

As you read on you will learn that there is so much to learn about being a Christian that there is no way I could possibly cover it all. God's wisdom is more than we can fathom. You will find it rewarding to continue your educational and spiritual growth as long as you persist in staying on course. Just like you need food every day to live, you need the word of God. The Bible is endless as far as the amount of knowledge you can gain from it. That is what makes it so amazing. There are folks that have been Christians most of their lives and they still continue to learn from it.

One of the reasons I used to criticize Christians when I was growing up was because I thought that people from Biblical times were easily influenced. Think of a young child, they are usually very naïve. You can tell them almost anything and they will believe it. I used to think that folks in earlier times were the same way. That history itself was not deep enough and people had not experienced much. For them to be told there was a God or that Jesus performed miracles was because they were naïve and gullible enough to not know the difference. Since I started reading the Bible, especially the book of Proverbs, I learned that the people of that time are just as smart as people today. You could make an argument that maybe even smarter. Smarter because they took the word of God seriously and truly lived by it. Probably more than people of modern times.

Why do you want to become a Christian? First of all, you need to understand what Christianity or being a

Christian means. A lot of people have a misconception of this. They think that being a Christian means that you are weak and get walked on by others. That they are passive and not capable of defending themselves. At least that is what I believed. Some people think of Christians as goody two shoes and never do anything wrong. That they go to church every Sunday to sing, pray, and listen to the pastor. A pastor that preaches on the consequences of how to live right or serve eternal damnation in hell. There is also a misunderstanding that Christians live double standards. A do as I say not as I do mentality. As you read on, these topics will come to light.

Before you can become a Christian, you have to believe with your whole heart that Jesus was born of the Virgin Mary. He is the Son of the Almighty God. that He died on the cross as a sacrifice to take on the sins of all mankind to allow man to have a relationship with God. You need to believe that he was resurrected three days later and now is sitting at the right-hand side of God. This is the entire basis of Christianity. This is why I feel that Easter needs to be celebrated more than Christmas. Yes Jesus' miracle birth is amazing. But what he did while on this Earth and why He died is truly more amazing and more meaningful.

If you do not believe any of this, then you will probably question everything else that is written in the Bible or what you were ever told. As well as you will struggle with your Christianity. The only way to conquer this hurdle is to start reading the Bible on a daily basis. Before you read, get on bended knee and ask God to show you the truth as well as an understanding of the scriptures you read. God, will never deny knowledge. I can promise you this; he wants a relationship with you, more than you want one with him.

When I started my transition, I believed in Jesus as well as I believed that he died on the cross. But there was something missing. I really cannot define what it was, except to say it wasn't a deep belief. One evening I had read the Bible, later on, I had gone grocery shopping. While I was shopping, I was reflecting on what I had read earlier. As I was gazing at a particular magazine on the rack. I do not remember exactly what I looked at. But whatever it was it reminded me of the movie "The Ten Commandments".

I had stated earlier that I watched this movie a lot as a kid and believed everything that took place. I wish I could tell you why I believed the life and times of Moses, but I can't. I just did. So, as I looked at this magazine, I thought to myself. "How much more relevant is Jesus than Moses"? Then it hit me like a ton of bricks. That Jesus and everything about Him is true. I was so excited about what I had come to realize that right there in the store I thanked God for showing me this. It all went back to asking God to show me what truth was.

One of my favorite scriptures is Romans 8:31 that says "If God be with you, who can be against you? That's a pretty powerful scripture. Basically, it says if God is in your corner, you will turn out victorious. I look at it as much more than that. To me, it means more than just winning. It means that God is willing to help you in so many ways. He wants to help you with whatever shortcomings you have, sins, and whatever else that may be controlling your life.
But I also believe it to come in the form of knowledge. The knowledge that makes you a stronger Christian. With knowledge comes power or strength. A strength that will give

you experience that God is with you. No matter what the circumstance, he will guide you through it. Lean on him for all things rather they be sins or lacking in faith. As you gain experience with Him, you will know that He will help you through every difficult situation in your life time and time again.

After reading the previous chapters, you probably have an understanding of what obstacles or key areas that I struggled with in my transformation. One of the hardest things was to understand sin and how it hurt my relationship with God. I had accepted Jesus Christ, prayed regularly, as well as I read the Bible daily. I started to notice a difference of having peace within myself. But there was still something not quite right. I was trying to rid all of the sin out of my life and I was not too sure how or if I could at all. Because I couldn't at first, I felt an emptiness. So, I began to research sin.

Now we all know this story. Adam was created by God. From Adam's rib, he made Eve. They lived in the Garden of Eden and had what most would consider a perfect life. They did not have to labor for their food, nor did they have any cares or worries. They were given instructions that they could eat from any tree in the garden except for the tree of the knowledge of good and evil. If they did, they would die. It was the disobedience of Eve that allowed her to be tempted by the devil disguised as a snake to eat the forbidden fruit. She was told that God was trying to keep Adam and her from knowing the difference between good and evil and that they would not die. If she ate the fruit she would be given knowledge as well as god-like powers and they would no longer need God. She ate from the fruit and then coerced Adam to eat from the fruit as well. God was so angry with them that he forced them out of the garden. This is how Satan works, he can take a little lie and it can become a huge mistake. I will discuss more of this later.

This event known as the "Original sin" changed the course of history where the spirit of man has been flawed. Because of that, we were all born with the nature to sin. This sin brought shame upon Adam and Eve. They discovered the feeling of guilt. They were ashamed of their nakedness and fled to clothe themselves with fig leaves as well as they tried to hide their faces from God.

They had to live in an area where they had to labor
for their food. They lost the place where all was provided
for them without having to work. They had to learn to
provide shelter for themselves. It has been said that
Eve discovered what pain was as she delivered the birth
of her children. Had she not sinned, she would have
had painless labor.

Because of what happened with Adam and Eve.
Cain and Abel, their two sons were also born with sinful
nature. Cain became a farmer and Abel was a
sheepherder. From the fruits of their labor, they were
commanded to make an offering. Abel offered the Lord
his best lamb. This was a lamb that was pure and
without blemish. God was pleased with Abel. Cain, on
the other hand, did not offer the Lord his best. God was
not pleased with him. Cain saw how pleased God was
with Abel that he became so jealous and outraged with
Abel, that he killed him. This was the first murder.
Cain's punishment was that he was forced to roam the
land without a place to call home. He was forced to
farm in a land that would not produce crops. He became
an outcast from God. It's obvious how sinning can cause

you much trouble. One sin can catapult into another then all of a sudden you are out of control and far away from having a relationship with God and his blessings. A simple little sin of jealousy can lead to murder. In fact, doesn't jealousy or envy usually lead to coveting or wrath, which can lead to murder? It is disturbing when you watch the news and learn of a murder. In a lot of cases, these murders were committed because someone was jealous of another for what they have. Their greed, lust, envy, or whatever brought them to this act.

You have to think that sin is like smoking. When you first start out it seems like there is no harm, no foul so you continue to do it over and over. After years of smoking, you discover that you have lost the battle. It has overtaken your life. You can't breathe as well as you used to, yet you continue to smoke. Then your lungs or your throat or both can become cancerous. They can be so cancerous that it could lead you to death. You were warned many times not to smoke. You wouldn't or couldn't stop. You depended on it to relieve stress, control your eating, or whatever reason you chose. It takes over your life, just like sin. You just can't stop. But I got good news for you. God can help you with all of this.

That is how sin can work in your life. You can start off by just telling a lie, which could seem harmless. Then that can lead to stealing, which from there can lead to more sins. That is where you need to have faith in God to ask Him to show you your sinful ways. Pray to Him and trust He will help you conquer that area in your life that needs to be corrected.

Sin can also be looked at as knowing what is right and not doing it, thus going against God's will. If you're in a situation where you might have doubt, trust that you shouldn't. More importantly, pray on it. You can be committing sins and not even know they are sins. After all, we are behaving in human nature. If you are unsure, ask God. He will show you.

When I looked at the areas where I needed improvement. Cussing and drinking were my first two issues that I chose to work on. I made a commitment to stop cussing for three days. It wasn't easy. After all, I used these words every day for most of my life. I once heard that if you did something for twenty-one days straight that it would become habit-forming. For instance, if someone wanted to stop smoking,   That if they made it for three weeks, then they would no longer have a desire to smoke. The same thing can be said for eating sweets or any other bad habit you want to kick or good habits that you want to pick up, such as reading the Bible daily.

Here I am at my first attempt to remove sin from my life. The three days would get conquered and then I would try for four days or maybe a week. I did not always make it. In fact, there were times I barely made it a couple of hours but I would keep trying. What I discovered was it wasn't so much the cussing. It was what led up to the cussing. You see the devil knew my weaknesses. All I needed was to get mad. Then I would start cussing like a river breaking through a levee. I felt so bad, that I had gone so long and would have to start all over again. Then guilt would set in. I used to think to myself that God would not bless me because I had used bad words. What took me a while to discover was that I was going through spiritual warfare. I will discuss more on that later. One thing that I was proud of was that I hardly used the Lord's name in vain. It was the other words that I struggled with.

Pay attention to what you are experiencing. Like I said earlier the devil knew my weaknesses. If I got mad, I would start cussing. I noticed that these times usually happened when I was tired. Now, think about this. When you are tired you are not as alert nor do you think as well as you normally do. Satan knew this with me and it seemed this was when he would do his best to attack me. He would bring things my way when I was tired, knowing what my reaction would be. Hoping that I would feel sorry for myself, not forgive myself and eventually turn my back on God and maybe turn away from Him completely. Now do not get me wrong I didn't adjust to him by sleeping more or becoming lazy. I just noticed it more and more. When situations occurred, I was getting wiser to Satan's tactics and would tell him he was not going to attack me this time.

Believe it or not, the drinking was easier than I thought. There became a time when the only time I would drink was while I was watching Nebraska football games. I then challenged myself to that as well and am proud to say that I went through the entire 2001 season without having one drink.

There is more to sin than cursing and drinking. I wanted to learn more, that took me to the Ten Commandments. They can be found in Exodus 20:1-17. God is so wonderful that he doesn't leave things for us to figure out on our own, He tells us. The commandments are laws that were given by God to Moses to pass on to the people of Israel. The first four commandments are laws directed towards God himself. The six that follow are directed towards man.

"Do not worship any other god". This means that God wants us to have a close and personal relationship with Him. He wants us to make Him the most important commitment, over anything or anyone else. He wants us to acknowledge that He is the Supreme Being. This is very important as well as probably one of the most overlooked sins. If you are doing anything in your life that keeps you away from him, you are breaking this commandment. This can include, sports, eating, or not attending church.

"Do not make false idols". To not worship anything or anybody other than God. This could mean money, your spouse, a celebrity, or even your favorite sports team. God is jealous and wants us to love Him for Who He is. Anything in our lives that keeps us away from Him either in the form of worship rather intentional or not goes against His will. To give you an example of this, shortly after the Israelites were rescued from Egypt they made a false god in the form of a bull made of gold and worshiped it. What was sad about this was that they were foolish. God, through Moses, rescued them from over 400 years of slavery from the Egyptians. While Moses was away on Mt. Sinai worshiping the Lord and receiving instructions. They forgot what he had done for them, got inpatient, made their own god, and praised it. We all can become guilty of this easily.

"Do not use the Lord's name in vain". This doesn't just cover saying the ultimate cuss word. It also warns about making promises in the Lord's name. You should never vow to do anything in the name of the Lord. A simple little phrase as "I swear to God" can be very harmful. You should not promise anything in the name of the Lord.

"Remember the Sabbath and keep it Holy". God created the world in six days. On the seventh, he rested. He commands us to do the same by not working on the Sabbath. By not doing this you are telling God you don't respect him. You could also look at it by saying you know more than He does and that you do not trust Him enough to provide for you. He made that day for us to not only rest but to worship Him.

"Honor thy mother and thy father". As you can imagine I had a tough time with this one. Despite all the turmoil in my childhood, I have to remember that God was with me all along and helped me get through it. So be thankful that you have parents rather they are your biological or adoptive. Do not judge them, thus you be judged. Don't criticize them either for what they did or didn't do. You have to remember that there is no instruction manual for raising children and some people just don't know how to be good parents. Know that you do have one perfect parent and that is your Heavenly

Father. Respect your earthly parents and help them in times of need. Remember this despite whatever happened they did provide for you.

"Do not murder". God created us, and it is up to Him when and how we should die. When we murder, we are trying to act like God by taking matters into our own hands determining someone else's fate. Remember what I said earlier about murder. Most murders are spun from another sin.

"Do not commit adultery". Marriage is a union between man and woman created by God. When you commit adultery you are disrespecting God by disrespecting your mate. The Bible teaches that when a husband and wife wed, they become one in the eyes of the Lord. When you cheat on your spouse, you are also cheating on yourself. More importantly, you are disrespecting God

"Do not steal". God will provide everything you need. To take from others tells God you are not showing faith in Him to provide you necessities such as money and food. If God provided it for your neighbor, it is not yours, so don't take it. Trust that He will not let you go without.

"Do not bear false witness against others". Be careful of what you say against one of God's people. By lying, it brings upon you and others a lot of unnecessary burdens. This also applies to gossip or spreading rumors. There is no better way to get into hot water with others than to spread gossip. The Bible, especially the book of Proverbs, tells how such a small thing like your tongue can get you into more trouble than you may realize. It is not wise to lie or gossip then praise God with the same tongue.

"Do not covet thy neighbor". Covet means to want what your neighbor has or to be jealous of what he has. If God has blessed your neighbor with more than what you have, that is between God and your neighbor. You do not know the relationship between the two and it is not your place to judge it. Instead of being jealous, be grateful that the Lord blessed your neighbor. Maybe the Lord will bless you as well, maybe through your neighbor. Or He may bless you with more than what your neighbor has. His timing is perfect and He has a reason for everything He does.

Sin can be summed up into one word, that word would be pride. Pride is the number one sin. Some would call it the root of evil. Being proud of an accomplishment or having pride in your children is one thing. Having pride that tells God that you are better than He is and that you can do all things without Him is completely different.

Pride was the single-handed sin that Satan committed that got him kicked out of Heaven. He was God's most powerful angel. He was perfect and beautiful in every way. He was also given a lot of authority. However, his pride got the best of him where he misused his power. He thought he could do all things better than God and wanted to be worshiped instead of God.   Ezekiel 28:14-19 tells of Satan's fall from grace.

The Bible states that if you committed adultery, you also committed murder. Basically, if you committed one sin, you have committed them all. To say that you are not a sinner or have not sinned is a pretty bold statement.

Proverbs 6:16-19 reads as follows: "There are six things the Lord hates, seven that are an abomination to him, haughty eyes, a lying tongue and hands that shed innocent blood, a heart that devices wicked plans, feet that make haste to run to evil, a false witness who breathes out lies and one who sows discords among brothers".

Galatians 5:19-21 says "Now the works of the flesh are evident: sexual immorality, impurity, sensuality, idolatry, enmity, strife, jealousy, fits of anger, rivalries, dissensions, divisions, envy, drunkenness, orgies and things like these. I warned you as I warned you before, that those who do such things will not inherit the kingdom of God".

Though the Bible does not call it these, we know these as the "Seven Deadly Sins". These sins of the flesh are greed, gluttony, envy, sloth, pride, lust, and wrath. Now there is a lot of speculation as to why they are called the "Deadly Sins". The Bible clearly states that no sin is worse than the other. These seven sins can collaborate along with the Ten Commandments.

The commandments when you really look at them are laws. Laws that were put in place by God to protect us from a path of self-destruction. Could you imagine what this world would be like if laws did not exist? We would have complete chaos. It would be survival of the fittest. Do you think we would have modern-day luxuries like are homes, electronics, automobiles, or whatever without laws? We would probably be living in a world more severe than third world countries struggling to eat and drink every day.

When people from the times of the Old Testament sinned; they would offer their best livestock to the Lord to ask for His forgiveness. This was the old Law of Moses. This practice would continue on all the way up until Jesus died on the cross. When he died it was considered the ultimate sacrifice, where man no longer had to sacrifice lambs or other livestock in an offering to God. Jesus was the ultimate sacrificial lamb.

Jesus died for all sins for all mankind. Think about that. Jesus loves us so much that he made the ultimate sacrifice to die for all of us in order that we can have a relationship with the Father and have eternal life. People who understand exactly what He did for all of us, know that no one has ever made such a huge sacrifice to so many. That is why He is worshiped and praised like He is. You know that I was a soldier in the Army. Though you cannot compare the two, many Americans are very thankful for all the soldiers that have fought for this country.

Especially those that gave their lives for us to have our freedoms. Well, Jesus did that for all of us to have freedom from sin and to have a personal relationship with God.

I sat back and thought about what good things came from my sins. I couldn't think of one. I drank a lot of beer. What did that do for me? It caused a lot of hangovers. I spent a lot of money, not to mention the damage I did to my liver or the number of brain cells I destroyed. I took a huge risk of drinking and driving. How many times did I cheat death or could have hurt or killed others? How many times did I get away with not being arrested for driving while intoxicated? Alcohol is nothing more than a fuel that sparks anger and you already know how many fights I got into.

I slept with women I shouldn't have, flirting with diseases and pregnancies. I spent many nights being ignorant and living on the edge. I am very fortunate that I never got into drugs. I can thank all of the stoners that I have met in my life for that. Stoned, drunk, and stupid are no way to spend your life.

Lying did nothing good for me. I didn't lie a lot compared to others that I know that would be called habitual liars. I do know that when I lied I hurt others as well as myself. Have you noticed that when you lie, you generally have to tell more lies to cover up the initial lie? Honestly (no pun intended) it is too much to keep up with. If you lie on a regular basis, people will have a tendency to not respect or trust you at all. I have known a couple of folks that have lied so much that they eventually believed their own lies and because of that, they had no sense of what the truth was anymore.

It took me a long time to finally realize that Nebraska football was not bigger than God. I bet that there are some people who know me would say that I worshiped Nebraska football like no other and I am sure God would consider it idolatry.

I used the Lord's name in vain but as I said earlier not as much as other cuss words. Regardless if I used it once or a million times. I did use it. God must truly love me, to forgive me for that. Not to mention how stupid and immature I must have looked because my vocabulary was very limited. I made it a point to not use foul language. I have noticed that people have more respect for me. I can remember carrying on conversations where others would cuss. Yet I refrained from using such language. You could just see the looks on their faces. Especially when they could tell that such a word was on the tip of my tongue and I caught myself. They would look at me with respect and probably thinking to themselves "He wanted to cuss but he didn't". I also noticed if someone knows you are a Christian and they cuss in front of you. They are more likely going to say they are sorry. Why do you suppose they did that? In my opinion, they were showing respect for me and my beliefs as well as they were showing their reverence to God.

There are other sins, like selfishness. I guess I could say I earned this one honestly as I was not given much as a child through affection or gifts. Because of that, I guess I did not know how to give of myself. So, I was very self-centered, it was always about me. Most of the "Seven Deadly Sins" are based on selfishness if not all of them.

I did cheat once in a while. You have probably heard of the old saying, "If you ain't cheating, you ain't trying". Well, how sweet is the reward if you had to cheat to get it. I didn't cheat that much, especially in my sports. I really didn't have to, but if I cheated at a board game, so what. Who cares? I won, or did I?

When I stole it was one of the dumbest I ever did. I never stole money, which was a good thing considering I worked most of my adult life as a manager. However, I did take things that weren't mine. Little things, but regardless they were not mine. One time when I stole, I had to lie to cover it. You see how one sin can lead to another.

During my senior year in high school, they changed the curriculum to where we had to take a semester of American Government. The teacher was one of my favorites. He was really cool. In fact, later in the year, he helped me out by writing the benediction, which is a prayer that I volunteered to read at the annual sports awards banquet. Imagine that, me, a non-Christian reading a prayer though I did not know who God was. You see, He was working in me before I knew it.

It was at the end of the semester, I was in the classroom and happened to notice a stack of tests on the teacher's desk for the upcoming final exam. It was so easy and the temptation kept tugging at me so I took one. Then through the aid of another student, I was able to get copies made up to hand out to anyone who asked for it. The sad truth is that because he was such a good teacher and I loved the American Government, there was no need for me to steal that test. I purposely missed one question so it wouldn't look obvious. I lied to cover up stealing a test that I would have aced. I can guarantee you my conscience was eating at me the entire time I was taking the test.

Now you should have a better understanding of sin and the repercussions that come from it. You may be asking yourself after all of the sins you have committed, "Can I still be saved?" The answer is "Yes, most definitely".

Chapter 7

Being Thankful

Every day, I am truly thankful for all God has blessed me with. When my life seemed to be worthless, it was God's word along with the kindness and love of His people that really helped me see the true beauty in life and all God's creations. I am extremely thankful that God had patience with me and that he never gave up. You should as well. God has given you more blessings than you are aware of. Hopefully, after you read this you will know exactly how much He loves you and has blessed you.

Though it may seem like there is an awful lot to do as a Christian, it really isn't. There is a lot to learn, but do not be discouraged. When you start learning you will discover that you will want to learn more. Plus, it is better to do things that are in accordance with God's will because without him it can and will be very hard. Remember Romans 8:31; "If God is for us, who can be against us"?

Like I have said earlier, Christianity can be compared to being on a diet. A diet is defined as a controlled intake of food, usually by someone who is trying to lose weight. Most people struggle with that. They have to make sacrifices that they are not used to or in some cases not willing to do wholeheartedly. There are others that consider a diet a lifestyle. They take it seriously enough to eat right, work out, and they feel better about themselves. To them, a diet has changed their life completely around and it seems almost effortless for them. Put your focus on God all day long as much as you can and try to make changes to your life. Just like those that watch what and how much they eat. He will guide you and direct you. He will talk to your heart and you will notice a difference. Make Him your lifestyle.

Why would you want to change your ways now instead of later? First of all, you can't be guaranteed tomorrow. There are many people who live a long time with a sin-filled life and never accepted Jesus until they were on their deathbed if at all. To me, that is pushing the envelope way too far. You cannot and should not question God and His timing. He is the creator of all of us. He decides when we are born and when we die. He is the potter and we are the clay. Only He can take a lump of clay like us and shape it into a beautiful piece of pottery.

If a person lives a long life full of sin, we may not know the circumstances of their lives as to why God was so gracious to allow them to live that long without accepting Jesus. He is a patient God and does not force us to love Him. He is also not going to give up on his people, yet that is still no reason to put him off. Those people should be thankful that He was kind and gave them that one last chance to accept Him before they passed.

Who are we to ever think that we will get that chance? Again, you cannot question God's timing. There are so many people that die and never get the chance to know Jesus. Think about someone who you may have known or read about in the newspaper that died in an automobile accident or some other tragedy. Do you think that person woke up that morning saying, "This will be the day that I die?" Probably not. Now,

how much more of a tragedy does it become if they had not accepted Jesus into their lives before
they died.

What if you are wrong about God and there is a Heaven and a Hell. What is the worst thing that can happen to you if you start living a Godly life? You will be living right, helping others that need it. All along gaining a good reputation and earning the respect of others. If you don't and end up going to Hell and eternal damnation. Is it worth it? Seriously, think about it.

Life is very precious and it is our responsibility to take it seriously enough to enjoy it. God's love for us is so awesome and it hurts Him when we do not accept Him. Think about how you would feel if you had a child that you loved and nurtured and he or she turned their back on you. That is what you are doing to God. That's why it hurts my heart when I hear of young people, especially those who have no consideration for their lives or the lives of others. They perform acts of stupidity or cruelty against themselves or others. Think about the innocent victims that are hurt or killed in these tragedies along with the pain and suffering that comes to their families.

These young men, who think they are so tough or so mean and perform these acts of cruelty, do not understand that they are going to probably spend the rest of their lives in jail. They feel somehow that they are glorified when all along they will be forgotten. If you are in your twenties and get sentenced to life, you could spend seventy-five percent of your life here on Earth behind bars. The crime you committed, was it really worth it?

Have you ever wondered why you see the elderly attending church more than the younger generations? Do you think it could be because they are thankful for the lives they have lived? That they have been through the difficult times in life, have matured and know who their creator is? Learn from them, you will be glad you did.

Again, why would you want to change your ways now? Remember we are not guaranteed tomorrow, but your life changes dramatically when you accept Jesus in your life. After I became a Christian, I used to joke that it was not time for me to die because God isn't through with me yet. It is a very boisterous statement. But because I have the knowledge of God and have accepted Jesus. It is a fair statement for me because I feel that God has a calling for me. I still don't know what it is quite yet, but I know there is something out there for me to do. It could be just keep on doing what I am doing now or I could be living it out right now in the form of writing this book. What I really mean is that I feel that He has a lot of work to do in me, to change my heart and my outlook in life. He has given me many talents and wants me to utilize them before it is time for me to go home and be with Him. Now if it is close to my time, I can say this. I like my chances a lot more of going to Heaven than I did before I was saved.

How do you get started in accepting Jesus? First of all, pray. Prayer is very important in establishing your relationship. Without prayer, your faith will not grow. In my opinion, you cannot have one without the other.

Simply ask Jesus to come into your life and forgive you for all your sins. Now, you need to make sure this is from your heart. You have to be truly sorry for the sins you committed. Not necessarily because of the problems they caused you, but that you went against

God's will. That you hurt people along the way.
Chances are you probably hurt one of his followers. You
may be asking yourself, "What if it isn't from the heart?"
Ask God to help you with that. To change how
you feel and how you act.

You should ask Him to teach you his ways. To not
only change your heart but your way of thinking, so that
you are able to act like he would in certain situations.
When Jesus was on this Earth, He sought after the
sinners and the sick. He cared for everyone. He loved
the sinner and not the sin. Matthew 9:9-13, He was
asked why he hung out with the sinners instead of the
righteous. He replied that "a well person doesn't need a
doctor, but a sick person does".

At first, when I used to pray, I was unsure of how to
pray or what to pray for. The Bible teaches that when
you pray, pray in the name of Jesus and through the
power of the Holy Spirit.

What does it mean to pray in the name of Jesus?
Jesus gave us full authority that when we pray to the
father and ask him for a blessing that if we do it in

Jesus' name, God will hear our prayer. It also means that we are glorifying Jesus himself. Going through the strength and power of the Holy Spirit means that we are asking the Holy Spirit to petition to God our requests. If you are
having a hard time with your words, the Holy Spirit will speak for you. Now, isn't that cool. An interpreter if you will. It also means that the Holy Spirit will plead for us in accordance with God's will.

Jesus said that we should pray the following way which is also known as "The Lord's Prayer". It has a significant meaning and should be used every day though it is not. It can be found in both Matthew 6:9-13 and Luke 11:2-4. Some believe that you should lead off every prayer this way while others believe it is just a template or pattern to use in prayer. My personal beliefs are that it needs to be a pattern so that we don't sound repetitious with our prayers or sound like some sort of incantation.

"Our Father who art in Heaven hallow be thy name". This acknowledges who God is, giving Him His glory

and respect as the creator of the Heavens and Earth.
He is to
be honored, with that, you will humble yourself in front of
Him. Just like if you were in front of a judge pleading
your case, what chances do you think you would have if
you did not show him any respect? The word "Hallow"
means to show great respect again
giving God our reverence for Him.

"Thy kingdom come thy will be done on earth as it is
in Heaven". This means that may all obey Him on Earth
as they do in Heaven. This is also asking Him to help
you to have the strength to obey Him

"Give us this day, our daily bread". This part is saying
thanks for allowing us to live another day and to provide
enough food for us to survive this day. It also means to
not give us more than what we need to not be a glutton
if you will.

"Forgive us our trespasses as we forgive those that
trespass against us". Here we are asking for forgiveness
for our sins. It is also asking us for help in forgiving
those that have sinned against us. Remember in order

for God to forgive you, you need to be able to forgive others first. More importantly, if you are like me, you need to learn how to forgive yourself.

"Lead us not into temptation, but deliver us from evil". We will always be tempted because Satan is always on the prowl. We are asking God to help us with those temptations that we do succumb to them. It is our free will or choice if you will to partake in any sort of temptation. We are asking God, to help us acknowledge the temptation and not to move forward with it. It is very important to know that temptation in itself is not a sin. Following through with it is. Know this; Jesus himself was tempted by Satan. So imagine if he can be tempted, so will you.

"For thy is the kingdom, the power, and the glory forever and ever, Amen". Again, giving God his glory and recognizing who He is. Recognizing that He is powerful and He through Jesus will defeat the enemy for good when they come.

There is something I need to inform you of when praying to God. First of all, He answers all prayers.

However, He doesn't always answer them when we would like Him to. His timing is always perfect. He sometimes answers "Yes" to prayers, sometimes He answers "No" or he may just simply say, "Wait". Just be patient and He will work things out for the better. There may also be times when He says "No" over and over. Instead of getting mad at him, ask yourself, or better yet ask Him, "Lord what am I doing wrong?" Or, ask Him "What is it, you want me to do"? Chances are you could be sinning or going against God's will.

Remember sin can separate you from God's blessings. You could also ask Him what he is trying to teach you. It is okay to question Him if it is enhancing your walk with Him. It could also be that other events have to fall in place first before you receive your request. When He says "No" you have to trust that he knows what is best for you. It is no different than when a parent tells a child "No". It's not that the parent doesn't love the child. He is just looking out for it.

There was a time when He kept telling me "No". As I look back at it, I am glad he did. When my daughter's mother and her left. I would pray non-stop all day that he brings them back to me. He did. But they were back only for that one day. Then I would pray over and over again for them to return. They didn't. After learning all I have, not just from this situation but from God as well. He knew that it wasn't good for us to be together.

When you ask Jesus to change your heart, practice being kind to others, go out of
your way to help. Speak words of kindness and show concern for your fellow man. Give to others and give of yourself. Stop being selfish, you will find how much smoother your days will become. You will begin to feel peace with others and more importantly with yourself.

For me, this wasn't an easy transformation. I still had a lot of bitterness in my heart. I also had a lot of anger. I had to ask Jesus to help me in these areas. There were days on end where I would be kind and courteous to everyone I met. Then all of a sudden, I'm mad at the world again. I expected to be changed permanently overnight and I wasn't. That made me mad. I later learned that I wasn't willing to make a complete change. I still had some bad habits I had to get rid of. I had a lot of resentment toward others who had hurt me or caused me problems. I wasn't willing to stop drinking completely, nor was I willing to give up some of my evil ways. I was still very opinionated and I had hatred in my heart. Because of my upbringing, this was a huge battle for me to conquer. You have to remember I was thirty-five years old when I first accepted Jesus into my life and so I had thirty-five years of training on how NOT to live like a Christian.

The point I am trying to make is that you have to learn from your mistakes. When you make a commitment to Him, do it with all you have and stay on course. Do not delay it by saying, "I'll think about it." You could be too late or certain events may occur that may harm you. Despite your feelings or emotions, stay true to your commitment. You will benefit from it. You will stumble or fall. That is alright, as long as you are willing to keep trying. God, knows what you have been through and doesn't expect perfection, but what is in your heart.

When you do pray, it should be done in privacy. This is personal time between God and you. Go to a secluded room in the house, close the door, and shut out all distractions; TVs, radios, whatever. Do not set a time limit. That's either showing off or disrespecting God. Meditate on your prayer before you start. Think about what it is you would like to talk to God about. Then pray. Be specific. For example: Let's say that you are looking for a different job. What kind of job? What is wrong with the one you have now? Do you want a better work

environment? Is it the pay? Tell God what it is exactly that you want different. Also, ask for His will in your life in this particular situation.   Ask for understanding or knowledge of the situation you are in and ask God what it is He is trying to teach you or how to see your way through it.

I find it best to pray in the morning and then again before I go to bed at night. However, there is nothing wrong with praying throughout the day. The reason why I find it best to pray in the morning is that it is the best way to get my day started and it shows God that I am putting Him first in my life. Then I would focus all day on that prayer.

Praying before I go to bed seems to always help me sleep more soundly. It gave me time to reflect on my day, ask for forgiveness for the sins I committed and mull over on the good things I did that day.

Praying is not to be a showcase. It is time for you to have a one-on-one relationship with God. You shouldn't brag that you pray, or how often you do it. As you pray throughout the day, you do not necessarily need to get on bended knee. Refusing to ever get on bended knee shows that you have no respect for God. There will be times
where you may have a need to pray while you are driving or any other instance where you just can't bend knees. You can also talk to God through thought or just a soft whisper.

Always give thanks for all you have, as well as give thanks for the trials and tribulations you are going through. If you are in a bad situation, it may be God who is allowing these things to happen to strengthen your faith. This is a progression period, which means He is working in you. He is teaching you something for whatever reason. Remember, no matter how rough you think you might have it, it could be worse. Chances are there is always someone else out there who has a situation worse than yours. I'm sure you have heard of the guy who complained he had no shoes until he met the guy with no feet.

I found it very handy to write out a list of everything I was thankful for by using each letter in the alphabet. When I gave thanks to God, sometimes I would refer to certain things on the list, or I would simply say, "You know everything I have on my list and I would like to take this time to give you thanks for all of it." It can be simple things or things of great importance.

My first list looked something like this: A- my attitude, B- the Bible, C- my career, D- my dog, E- my enthusiasm and energy towards Him, F- my friends, G- God, Himself, H- my home, I-my intelligence and integrity I was gaining through my walk with Him J- Jesus, K- kindness He has shown me, L-love He has given me, M-my maturity, N-Nebraska football, O- the great outdoors, P- my pastor, Q- my quenching for Him, R-reflecting on His word S- my salvation, T- His timing, which is always perfect. U-United States of

America, V-Victory in Jesus, W-wisdom, and my wife. X- Nothing for this one (there aren't too many words beginning with X), Y- my youthful heart, Z-zoos, because I love animals so much. You see almost anything can be used to give thanks for.

This list should change as you grow in your relationship with God. You will discover how many more things you are grateful for. You can have more than one thing for each letter if you want. Seriously, the more you are thankful for, the closer your relationship with God will become. When you do this you will realize that you truly do have a lot to be thankful for. It will make you wonder why you ever complained about your life in the first place.

Pray for others. Sit back and think of people you know that are not well and could use his healing touch. Pray for those who do not know Him, that they may receive Jesus into their hearts. After a while you may discover that you are praying more for others than yourself, if at all. That is Spiritual growth at its finest.

You can make a prayer list by writing down the names of those you would like God to bless either in healing or of the Holy Spirit. You can have a list of situations, which you may want God to work in for you. I found this to be a very useful tool. For one, I didn't want to be repetitive in my prayers. Two, I didn't want to be long-winded. Three, I didn't want to leave anyone or any one thing out.

Finally, talk to Him and ask Him for your blessings. There is something you need to remember though. His timing isn't always the same as ours. As well as he may not always say "Yes" he could also tell you to wait. I can speak very highly of this as He has gotten me through many obstacles and not necessarily when I wanted him to. But, it always turned out better than I had hoped. There is a reason for everything He does. Sometimes we understand, others we don't. Remember we are the clay and he is the potter. He is molding us into our very best.

It seems like an awful lot to do, to pray every day at least once. But it really isn't. Nor is it a lot to try to remember. In the beginning, keep it simple. God knows what you are going through. Remember he wants this relationship more than you do. He is a patient God.

One time when I was praying to God, I was really feeling at one with him. I was sitting alone in a park. After my prayer time, I heard the most beautiful sound. Something I have never heard before or since. There was a flock of birds that flew over my head. They were high enough that I couldn't tell they were coming but yet low enough that once they were overhead, all I could hear was the flutter of their wings. It was truly an amazing sound. I sat back in awe and looked up to God to thank Him. I knew that he heard my prayer and He was letting me know.

I can also remember this one time when I was having a busy day at work and had this terrible headache. Just like most illnesses they always seem to come at the worst possible time. Not even thinking about it, I went to the restroom, got on my knees in front of the sink, and prayed to God to please make my headache go away. As I got up, my headache was gone. I was so excited, scared, and shocked all at the same time. It was the first prayer that God had answered for me on the spot. I will never forget that moment as long as I live. It's amazing how a simple thing as a headache can draw you closer to God.

When you start your relationship with God, it is best if you can remain teachable. You need to have an open mind and not reject what you are being taught as opposed to learning it with all you have. It is one thing to hear the message or read the Bible, but when the Bible tells you how to live. It is best if you try to apply your teachings to your everyday way of life. Don't be discouraged when God corrects you either. He corrects those he loves. It is the same if you don't like it when your kids get upset when you are correcting them.

When you read the Bible, select a certain book or series of books. Then, before you read, ask God for knowledge and understanding. I started off reading the gospels. The gospels are Matthew, Mark, Luke, and John. They are the first four books in the New Testament and cover the life and times of Jesus. They set the table for Christianity. In these books, you will discover parables. Parables are stories that Jesus spoke of that taught morals and values. They are an analogy of certain situations. To me, the Gospels were very helpful in understanding who Jesus really is and all He did and went through leading up to his crucifixion.

I followed up with the remainder of the New Testament. Most of the books of the New Testament were written by the Apostle Paul. His books give instructions on how to live a Holy life. He gives hope and understanding as well as warns you about straying from the word of God. These books gave me so many uplifting feelings that it helped me stay on the course I needed to.

The Old Testament tells of the early years of mankind. It starts off with God creating the Heavens and Earth as well as the creation of Adam and Eve. It details the lives of Noah, Abraham, and Moses and his aiding of the Jews in exiting Egypt. Kings Solomon and David are also mentioned. There is so much there. It all leads up to the birth of Christ. I'm not going to lie to you, following the Old Testament can be hard. There is so much history to it and at times it will give a complete list of ancestors and will
leave you feeling like you need to draw out a family tree.

There are so many amazing things in the Bible. If you really want to learn about how to improve yourself, read the book of Proverbs. It is mostly written by King Solomon, who is considered the smartest man ever. It is a book of wisdom. It is a book that tells you what you should and should not do in order to live a Holy life. It tells you how not to be angry, how to not run your mouth, and how to treat others. When I first read it, I thought to myself, "Man, am I in trouble!" I used to think that book was written specifically for me.

Just like praying, don't try to limit yourself to how long you should read or how many chapters you should read. When you set a time frame, you are telling God, this is all the time I am allowing for you today. When you set a limit to the amount of chapters or verses, you may not get the knowledge or understanding that God is trying to give you. The Bible is God's word, which is food for the soul, so read until you are full.

Don't be like me before I was a Christian and criticize it, especially if you don't know anything about it and its contents. The Bible is a wonderful book. It is a history book as most of the Old Testament will show you. It is an instructional book. The book of Proverbs will educate you on so much, as will the writings of Paul in the New Testament.

It is a book of hope and love as the stories told by Jesus will show. His teachings and parables are fascinating. The love that He shows for His disciples and other followers is genuine. He showed so much affection for others that it was immeasurable. He would travel great distances to heal the sick and forgive the sinners. He cast out demons from the possessed. His devotion to God is colossal. He tells you how to have a personal relationship with God.

It is a book of sorrow and triumph and it tells how Moses rescued the Jews out of Egypt and how they roamed the desert for forty years until they reached the Promised Land. It is a book of faith. It tells how Abraham was willing to sacrifice his only son as worship to God. God was impressed by his faith and allowed his son Isaac to live. The book of Job, tells the story of how one man lost his entire fortune and family yet, he knew that God would see him through.

It is a book of truth. The entire book was written by God through people he chose to be its authors. I was once told that in order to believe the Holy Bible you have to believe everything in it, cover to cover. It is an inspirational book. Almost anywhere you look in the New Testament, there are words of encouragement. Words that will make you feel good about yourself and give you hope to face and conquer any obstacle or fork in the road you may encounter.

It is a book of morality. Jesus' parables tell you how to handle certain situations or how to think properly. It is because of His life, that the bumper stickers WWJD, (What Would Jesus Do?) became so popular. Jesus wants you to live and think as He did. To have enough faith in God, that you could move a mountain.

It is timeless, no matter how long you read it; you will always learn something new from it. You could read scripture to help see yourself through a certain situation, then later down the road that same scripture can have a different meaning to help you with a completely different situation. What other books can do that?

It is a book of knowledge. You will never learn everything it has to offer. I once heard that the more worn that the Bible is from being used, the cleaner the heart and soul. It is truly amazing. It is not by accident that it is the all-time number one selling book in the world.

My first Bible was very helpful to me. In front of it, it had a list of scriptures to help me through all sorts of topics in life. Such as dealing with depression, loneliness, stress as well as understanding God's will for me in my life, and seeking forgiveness. It has helpful tips in so many areas. It has a section congratulating me on the purchase of it. It says that if I use it correctly it will not only change my life but assist in building my relationship with God. How many books can make that claim?

I had a tough time with my transformation. It is very possible that you will also. Let me ask you this: Have you ever wanted something so bad, that you worked very hard to get it? It could be anything such as saving money for a new car, studying hard for a test, training to win an athletic contest. How wonderful did you feel when you obtained your goal? I bet you were very proud. How proud would you have been, if it was just handed to you? The prize wouldn't have been as sweet. The glory that goes with it wouldn't have been as nice. So, stay the course.

Here is a test that I use to perform on myself in order to help me be more tolerant of others and how others may conceive me. I used this tool to improve my walk with the Lord. You know that road rage is sweeping the nation right now. Nothing would make me madder than the driving habits of others. In fact, it was usually one thing or another that would upset me and then all of the other things that bother me resurfaced and I found myself falling away from God. The following is a list of driving habits that I incorporated that can be very helpful.

When I drove on the interstate, nothing made me madder when someone was in such a hurry. They would ignore or could care less where I was, change lanes in front or back of me, and get really close to hitting my bumper. Especially if they did so without using their turn signal. I would use to cuss them out and let them know they were number one.

What I would do to counteract this, I always made sure that I always used my turn signal. I would make sure that if I changed lanes I did so with plenty of clearance. I was showing acts of kindness hoping they would notice and pass it on. I noticed that I became more aware of the road and those around me. Kind of like how I became aware of Satan and the attacks he could have on me. If I could sense other drivers would change lanes without using their signal, I would adjust my speed to allow them to get over. If they used their signal, I would respond by flashing my bright lights, letting them know I acknowledge them, and am allowing them to get over.

If I was unaware of someone and they nearly clipped the front end of my car. Instead of getting mad or speeding up to not allow them over. I would simply wave at them as to say I am not going to allow you to affect me, and you have a nice day anyway. By doing this, I was showing that I would be kind to others regardless of the offense they did against me.

After all, do I really know what is going on in their life and why they are in such a hurry? Granted they could be just a jerk on the road. But what if there was a true emergency? Did I really need to judge them? So I became more considerate of their needs or problems.

Then I practiced driving the speed limit and watching others pass me by. This taught me patience and discipline. Patience in that I would get to my destination. Discipline, that if I was organized and left on time or ahead of time so I would get to my destination on time or early. I stayed in my lane as opposed to jumping from lane to lane. This helped me stay on the narrow road to success and trust God. Just like the Bible teaches.

By applying the rules of the road, I found myself applying the laws of God more in my life. I drove the speed limit and trusted him. I stayed in the lane of righteousness. I didn't judge others, not knowing completely what they were going through. The more I applied these rules, the more I saw those around me following the same rules and being more considerate on the roads. Tell me God isn't awesome.

Be creative with your own ideas and then you will realize that the lessons you apply on the road will start applying to other matters in your life. You too can see how wonderful He is. If God is on your side, and if you are on His, He will help you see your way through anything.

Make a commitment to go to church every Sunday and try to go to Bible study. It is helpful because it has a question and answer format, something you don't do during a service. Dedicate time every day to reading the Bible even if it is for ten to twenty minutes and pray whenever you feel the need.

Over a period of time, you will notice a change in how you behave, feel, and think. God's power will have a very spectacular warmth that will travel through your entire body. It is a feeling of peace. You will discover that the things that bothered you before, no longer do. If you have a temper, it will eventually decrease. The desires of your heart will change. You will change in ways that you didn't know exist.

It wasn't easy giving up going to the bars or hanging out with my friends. It wasn't easy to stop swearing or saying negative things about others. It was extremely difficult to remove the anger in my heart. I had a lot of resentment towards all those that opposed me and caused me great grief.

That was when I had to reach deep down inside and say over and over that I forgive those who hurt me. It took a while. I think a lot of it was because I still had a quick temper and all I had to do was think about those events and my anger evolved all over again. When that happened, I found myself not forgiving them once more. We have the ability to forgive and we really need to do so. Unfortunately, we do not have the ability to forget. This is where you can ask God to help you. When you reach that point, I cannot explain enough how wonderful you will feel. It is like the biggest burden has been lifted off of your shoulders. You will feel better in so many ways. It is not an accident when you see Christians who are in much better health or seem to have that glow emanating from their faces. It is because they have Jesus in their lives and the Holy Spirit in their hearts.

The devil has a way of messing with your head. You will find that the mind is a battlefield. Don't be like people of this world who do not ask God to help them change the way they think. The devil will try to put bad thoughts in your head. He will try to get others to cause you grief. He will do everything, and I do mean everything, to turn you away from the Lord. 1 Peter 5:8-9 says. "Be on guard and stay awake". Your enemy the devil is like a roaring lion, sneaking around to find someone to attack. But you must resist the devil and stay strong in your faith". When I was in the Army, they taught us in order to defeat the enemy, you have to know the enemy. No truer words have ever been spoken.

You will ask yourself if this is really worth it. The answer is "Yes, most definitely." Jesus himself suffered, and look where he is now…He is sitting on the right side of God. You will also ask yourself, "When I was a sinner, why wasn't my mind so bogged down?' This answer comes in two parts. First, you were a sinner and

Satan had you where he wanted you. The second is that you didn't know God, and he doesn't force you to praise Him or follow Him. He gives us free will. If you want his favors, you need to accept Him as your Lord and Savior and break away from your sinful ways. I can promise you with all certainty that the prize the Lord has in store for you is greater than anything on this Earth you could ever receive. Over a period of time, your mind will not be overwhelmed. In fact, it will be more relaxed than you can imagine.

When I first started my transformation, I felt lost and scared. The first time I went to church, I cried and cried hard. That was nothing to be afraid of as that was the Holy Spirit working in me. Forgiving me for all my sins and comforting me into the arms of God, just as I had asked for. I couldn't understand how grown men whom I have never met before reached out and gave me a hug. You could tell that God was working through them by giving me a hug filled with love and understanding. Most importantly assurance that everything was going to be alright. It was scary just like any change in your life. Just know that God does not hate you. He loves you and is always ready to welcome you into His arms. I had a hard time believing that I could be loved as much as God loves me. He cares for us so much that He knows how many hairs are on our heads.

I felt so lost because I was unsure of what my future with God would be like. I wanted to know Him and not judge Him as I had in the past. I was unsure if He would forgive me of my sins. I was a misled boy but I always felt I had a good heart. I asked myself if He could really love me for what I was like before. The answer is, He loves all of us and is so willing to have us and forgive us. I had to learn to stay away from the laws of the world and realize that the devil was trying to ruin me. I was on a fast track to destruction.

Once you start your routine with everything I have mentioned thus far. You will notice a change in yourself. You will start having more peace in your heart and things that used to bother you, no longer will or at least not as much.

Chapter 8

The Five "F's"

I would like to discuss faith, forgiveness, fellowship, fasting, and free will in this chapter. I didn't plan it this way, but this could also be called the five "F's" of Christianity. They are the basics of having a relationship with God. To strengthen that relationship, you need to develop your faith in Him, and when you do you will develop trust. You will also need to learn how to be forgiving as God wants us to be. The fellowship is what you need to strengthen your relationship with God in understanding Him through the body of Christ of fellow Christians. Then there is understanding why you would want to fast and how to do it. Lastly, free will and why it is so important that God gave it to us.

I want to bring this point up again because I feel it is very important. There are people that question God's existence or the contents in the Bible. I have two questions for those types of people. What if you are wrong? What is the worst that can happen to you by following the laws of God? Let's say there isn't a Heaven or a Hell. But you follow the guidelines that God has laid out for you. You live a meaningful life and are well respected.

Now let us say there is a Heaven and a Hell and you refuse to live by God's standards. It seems like an awfully big risk not knowing what can happen to you after you die or even before you die. If there is a Heaven and Hell and you choose not to follow the laws of God and end up in eternal damnation. Are you willing to take that risk?

No matter how much you may learn from this text, I encourage you to learn more on your own. There is so much to learn about being a Christian. It can be so exciting and by no means is it difficult as long as you are willing to learn and give one hundred percent. You may want to seek advice from a pastor or maybe a fellow Christian. Do not be intimidated by pastors or feel that you can't talk to them. They are there to help and it is their job to guide you. Never stop learning or you will stop growing.

One of the best ways to tackle these areas is to put God first in everything you do. How do you do that? First of all, start by developing a relationship with Him through prayer and spend time reading the Bible. As you do that daily you start to become more conscientious of the word of God. You will then start feeling his presence in everything you do. I like to pretend that no matter what I did or what I said. I had to act as if He was right there next to me. Honestly, He is.

Look at it this way. What if you were at a function such as a wedding or a birthday party. There happens to be a priest there. How would you conduct yourself in his presence? Would you cuss or carry on as you normally would? Probably not. Since God is everywhere. When you go through your daily routine, always remember that He is right there with you. When you are confronted with a situation where you may find yourself acting like the old you, stop yourself and ask, "How would I act if God were standing right next to me?"

In the last chapter, I discussed how the devil is always on the attack. To help your faith in the Lord grow, you also need to know how the devil works.

Remember how I told you when I was in the Army they taught us how we had to know the enemy in order to defeat the enemy? He will do anything to disrupt your faith in the Lord. If God is alive and well, you also have to know that the devil is too. For everything good, it is opposed by evil. Satan is the master deceiver. He will stop at nothing to throw you off track, more so in the early stages of your Christianity.

As God teaches you how He works and is instilling faith and trust in you, remember to have patience, not only with yourself but with God. Your transformation will not happen overnight. You may lose a few battles along the way, but know that you will ultimately win the war.

In the early days of my Christianity, I had so many ups and downs that I couldn't keep count. Reflecting on those days, I can only think that most of that rollercoaster ride was of my own doing. It was because I had not learned every aspect of the devil attacking me. I was letting him into my life by allowing the little things to get to me. Things such as my temper, revisiting past moments, and not committing myself completely to the Lord.

The devil knows your weaknesses better than you do. One of mine was when I was tired, after a long day, my strength grew weary, so would my faith. I would question things such as how good was my relationship with God. The devil knew this. That was when he did his best work in me. He would have me believe all sorts of things against God and His will for me in my life. He would put bad thoughts in my head, have me feeling unforgivable, or would stir up anger from things in my past. Therefore, I would stop forgiving those that I forgave before.

Faith is not an emotion; it is a state of mind and a feeling in your heart. If I was well-rested and alert, I knew that my faith was strong. I could feel the Holy Spirit working in me and for me. When I grew tired and weary, my guard was down and the devil would oppose me and make me feel unworthy of God's forgiveness and love.

Another way the devil worked in me, was he had a way of instilling fear. He had me believe that I was unable to do what I thought I needed to do, or what God wanted me to do. He would have me feel that God was not there for me. That I was such a horrible sinner, that I didn't deserve anything I asked for and that God didn't love me.

I was allowing the devil to get the best of me. Satan will do anything to make your life miserable. He will attack you in ways that you wouldn't imagine. He will try to provoke you through others. He will tempt you in every way possible. He knows what triggers your emotions and will get others to tempt you. You will then show signs of anger, envy, and so forth. Regardless of the emotion, he has won.

I can think of several times when he used people to get the best of me through provocations. I would lose my temper, say, or do something that was not right. The guilt would consume me and I was unable to forgive myself let alone ask God for forgiveness.

When this happened to me, I had to realize that I was falling away from God. Or was I? God knew what was going on. I at the time didn't. Nonetheless, I stayed the course and would continue praying, asking for forgiveness, and read the Bible with a vengeance.

Everything would be alright for a while, and then it would start all over again. It was through these experiences that I learned what Satan was trying to do. Now, it does not affect me, or not as much as it did before.

I am not trying to scare you, but when you become a Christian, there will be spiritual warfare. This is a battle between God and the devil for your soul. God is very pleased that you are accepting him. Satan, on the other hand, will try to discourage you from the truth of God's ways. He will let you believe that you can sin and that God will be ok with that. The next thing you know, one sin leads to another and suddenly you spiral out of control.

What is faith? Faith is believing, without seeing. It is knowing that you are going to receive the graces of God's blessings. It is knowing that through your relationship with the Father that you will have eternal life. Faith is trusting God to handle all of your situations for you. It is about praying to Him on all things and knowing He will work them out for the good. It is knowing that God will protect you from the forces of evil. It is knowing that Jesus died on the cross for our sins;

that His blood was the ultimate sacrifice. His death served as a bridge to close the gap between God and us. Faith is putting your trust in God that He loves you so much and He wants what is best for you.

I once had a friend describe to me that faith is believing that the events that took place in the Bible are true and indisputable. We were taught in school that the Revolutionary war took place though none of us were around to witness it. Yet, we believed it to be true. Therefore, since the Bible is a history book and certain events were recorded. Then it is safe to say as Christians we should believe that what we read is the truth.

It took me a while to understand even though I believed in God, my faith in Him for my situation wasn't that strong. I believed He was the Almighty, the Creator of the Heavens and the Earth. I believed a lot of things about Him, except I had very little faith in Him to answer my prayers. Not so much the little things like helping me with a headache, but more along the lines of the bigger issues. I did, however, have faith in Him when I prayed for others. That was not a problem for me because it wasn't for me directly. Because I was never shown much love as a child I couldn't understand how someone could love me, considering my past. These feelings were coming from the devil and making me feel I was unworthy.

I couldn't stop sinning either. I thought it was okay to go out and party as long as I asked for forgiveness. I learned the hard way that forgiveness was not a license to sin. You truly need to live every day as a Christian. You have to make the adjustment to live your life as a Christian would. Just like the bumper stickers that have "WWJD" on them. "What Would Jesus Do"? Would Jesus go to a nightclub and party the night away? No! Would He get into a fight and punch someone out? No! So, we are to live and model our lives just like Him. I don't know how long it took me to realize that but when I did, I noticed my life became more joyful and more meaningful. I started to believe I had a purpose. I started to trust God that there was more fun in life than to keep doing what I was doing.

You may ask yourself if God loves you so much, why would He allow the rollercoaster ride that you will go on.

He does this to test your faith. He wants you to know that when things look bleak, that is when He is at His best. He wants you to always have hope, no matter what the situation. Through this, you will learn to trust Him in all things and after a while you will have such trust and respect for Him that your ground will not be shaken anymore. You will realize that God has gotten you through so many things in the past, and again He will prevail for you.

There was this time when I was on a flight to Chicago. As we were approaching the airport, the pilot told us we were going to have a delay in our landing. It seemed that the weather was backing up the traffic. Looking out the window, all I could see was a bright sun and the normal cloud coverage when you are up that high. I was thinking to myself that this can't be much of a storm. When we descended below the clouds, I could see how nasty the weather was. We eventually landed. Once we took off again and soared above the clouds, there was the bright sun again. That was when it hit me; this is exactly how God works. Even on the gloomiest of days when all seems useless and dark, that is when He is at his best. You can't see it until you rise above the clouds.

I cannot emphasize how important it is to pray every day and read the Bible as much as you can and learn from it. Don't be like some and read it just to read it or go through the motions. Learn it, understand it, and let it soak in. Don't read it to just find out what's in it for you. Yes, there are rewards for you but it's more than that you have to live it. It is better at times to just read a couple of scriptures over and over again and reflect on them. Read them out loud, so that you can hear what you are reading to help it soak in. The Bible is a wonderful book. Like I mentioned before, it is a history book, it is an instructional book. It is a book of hope and love. It is a book of truth. It is a book of sorrow and triumph. It is an inspirational book. It is a book of morality. It is timeless and most of all it is a book of everlasting knowledge.

Go to church, not just when you feel like it, make it a habit. You will later discover that you can't wait to go back. God's word will leave you hungry for more. Learn as much as you can and apply what you learn to your life. This will also help you develop your faith. Notice how others in church behave. Model yourself after them. The next thing you know, you will be acting just like them. You will feel better inside and have a look on your face that others will notice.

Take notes. The first church I attended, the pastor had us flipping pages in the Bible so much that I had to take notes just to keep up with him. I found those notes very useful because I would read them over and over throughout the week. Have you ever noticed when you take notes you are more prone to learn?

The Sundays I went to church and listened profoundly to the powerful messages from the pastor, I noticed how much better my weeks went. I was elated throughout the entire week. It was God, using the Holy Spirit to talk to my heart. I would get so excited that I wanted more. I would read my notes, listen to the tape of the sermon over and over. I couldn't wait to go next week. You can see what can happen if you don't go to service regularly. You could miss something very important that God is trying to teach you. Knowledge is good. I noticed the Sunday's I didn't go; I usually struggled through the week. Not that it would be a bad week, but it sure wasn't as smooth as the weeks when I went.

I went so far as to watch certain television evangelists. Joyce Meyer, Joel Osteen, and Charles Stanley ended up being my favorites. I watched others such as Creflo Dollar, Jerry Hagge, and Michael Yousef, to name a few. They all had a way of just saying things that made me think about my life. They had such an impact on my spiritual growth that I started a video library of their services. That way I could go back and watch them anytime I felt the need.

This brings up something that I always found truly amazing with the relationship I was developing with God. It seemed that whatever area I was struggling within my life, the pastor would discuss that in his message on Sunday. Then in a different light, Joyce, Joel, and or Charles would also discuss that same topic on their television programs usually in the same week. I could not believe how many times this happened. It was truly God trying to get a message to me through others.

Again, I was developing my faith in Him. God can and does work in many mysterious and wonderful ways.

One particular Sunday at church, the pastor was talking about how forgiveness was not a license to sin. The same week, I watched Joyce, Joel, and Charles and they all had a message very similar to that. That was God talking to me, telling me to get that out of my system. Thus, he was developing my faith in Him. He was showing me His work and how much He cared for me.

If you are not sure which direction God is trying to lead you, or you want to deepen your faith with him. Of course, you can pray for it or you can fast. Fasting is a concept where you are telling God that you are going to discipline yourself by eliminating something in your life for some time. It is giving God reverence as well as telling Him that you are willing to make a sacrifice for Him. Many people fast from certain food groups.

The word "Breakfast" comes from the meaning of breaking your fast from the previous day's meals or supper. When you think about it, you usually eat three times a day roughly over a ten to twelve hour period. When you eat breakfast the following day you will have gone again ten to twelve hours between meals, thus you are breaking a fast.

Fasting can come in many forms. You can fast from watching television or from hanging out with your friends or anything else that would show discipline on your behalf and giving that time to the Lord. Some folks fast as a dedication to God. They are showing Him that they want to take their relationship with Him to the next level and that they are thankful for what they already have. I have found this as a wonderful way to strengthen your faith as any other.

Because I am such a sports fanatic, I could get caught up in just about any game that was on television fairly easy. But there was this time that I felt I needed to fast. I prayed to God to tell him that I was going to give up television every night for two weeks up until 10 p.m. I chose that time as I also felt that it was important for me to catch up on the late evening news. What I did during those times when I normally would have watched a ball game, I read the Bible, I prayed and most importantly I just sat back and listened to God speak to my heart.

Some people fast until they receive a sign from God pertaining to a certain situation in their lives. There is nothing wrong with that as long as it is for a good reason and bringing them closer to Him. However, I want to warn you about asking for signs. People tend to ask God for a sign for various reasons. The Bible teaches to not ask God for a sign because it may show that you are testing Him. He will give you signs. My experiences have taught me that. They have come when they are not asked for. In some cases, it has been God telling me or showing me what to do. Either, in my thoughts, dreams, or touching my heart, like he did with me to write this book. Trust me; He will give you a sign when the time is right. Just like after my prayer when I was sitting in the park and I heard the flutter of the birds' wings. He was telling me He heard my prayer.

I used to ask God whether or not He was going to allow my daughter and her mother to come back into my life. His perfect number is seven. I would ask him to show me three sevens in a row like in the form of a phone number or license plate number before I reached a certain destination or time of the day. I used to drive myself nuts looking for these numbers. So much, that it's a wonder I didn't get into an accident. I would see the numbers sometimes and at times almost immediately. Other times not at all. I was asking God for signs and driving myself crazy in the process as almost like I was willing Him to give me what I wanted. God doesn't work that way. I realized that I was questioning my faith in Him. More than that was I allowing Satan a crease to get into my life.

If you are at that crossroads and are looking for an answer from God and confused about his answer. I have found it best to ask Him to tell me what to do through other people. If I had a particular question that I wanted to be answered. I would ask the Lord to speak to me through my pastor or Sunday school teacher. I found it to be very effective. Generally, this has worked when I feel that God may be trying to teach me something, and I just couldn't quite figure it out.

In the last chapter, I had mentioned how God answers prayers. When I said that he says "No" sometimes, it is because He loves us. He knows what's good for us. When I was asking Him to bring my daughter and her mother back into my life, he kept saying "No". As I look back on those days, I am very glad he did. I can almost guarantee you that my life would still be in chaos. My walk with the Lord would probably not be as strong, or maybe not at all.

Imagine yourself as a parent. Let's say that your child asks you for something that you know isn't good for them. Do you tell them "Yes" to give them their way knowing the outcome? You might use it as a tool to teach them. But more than likely you are going to tell them "No" because you love them so much and you do not want to see them get hurt. That is how God operates. Through this, we learn to establish more faith in Him.

One thing that took me a long time to learn was patience. When I talk about the rollercoaster ride I went on, let me tell you this had been one crazy ride. We live in an instant society now, God doesn't. Sometimes I had to learn the hard way that God's timing is not our timing and that His timing is never late. I cannot begin to tell you how many times I prayed for something with a time frame and it never happened. I learned that if you stay on course with God and do your best every day, He will reward you with what your heart desires. He works in wonderful ways. His timing is when you least expect it and ends up better than you hoped for. Patience and faith are almost hands in hand.

For example, I was up for a promotion. I thought I had it in the bag. Well, after my review with the company owner. I learned that I was not getting the promotion. Needless, to say I was devastated. My boss, a Christian man himself saw the look on my face. He responded by saying "You know when God closes a door, another one opens". They were nice words, but I wasn't buying it at the time. Five weeks later, I was called by him and wouldn't you know it, I got a promotion. Better yet, I was heading to Lincoln, Nebraska the home of my beloved Huskers as opposed to the previous position sending me to Council Bluffs, Iowa. Wouldn't you know it; I got another promotion less than a year later. I can almost guarantee that opportunity would not have been available if I was promoted the first time.

Another way to build your faith is to tithe. The word "Tithe" is an old Hebrew word meaning ten percent. The Bible speaks of tithing when making offerings to the Lord. I truly believe in this. Give the Lord ten percent of your earnings and he will reward you abundantly. After all, everything is His. It is alright to tithe to show God that you trust Him for greater wealth. But at the same time, it can't be for the love of money. Money in itself is not evil, however, the love of it is. Remember you can't serve two gods. Serving money over God is idolatry. Some people tithe, because they are thankful for what the Lord has given them and they give it in thanks to Him for what they have been blessed with. I believe that if you tithe it is an offering of thanks. That speaks highly of what is truly in your heart. After all, isn't it better to give than to receive? The word abundance can mean so much more than wealth. It could mean blessings in many other ways such as good health or others.

Look at faith from a different perspective. Every day you sit in the same chair and every day it supports you. But not once since the day you bought it, did you ever wonder if it was going to hold you up. How many mornings have you gone out to your car and wondered if it was going to startup? In both instances, you took it for granted that both items would perform their assigned function. Why would you question your faith in God?

Faith is not a religion. Religion is a sect with certain beliefs or views. Rather it is Christianity, Muslim or Buddhist. Faith is the personal relationship you have with God. It is trusting him in every aspect of your life. People may ask you what church you belong to, that is fine. They may even ask you how deep your faith is. None of that matters with God. It does, but it doesn't. He does not necessarily want you to be a member of a church as much as He wants that one on one with you. Don't get me wrong. The church is important, it's where you develop fellowship, you praise Him with others and you receive his good word. Even though you can get it from the Bible, it is nice to have a pastor break down scripture in layman's terms or help you see things from a different perspective.

God will allow certain things in your life that may not seem fair. He does this so we will learn to glorify Him when things look bleak. We learn to rely on Him and He shows us time and time again that he will get us through those cloudy days and will always do so. Deuteronomy 31:6 says "Be strong and courageous. Do not be afraid or terrified because of them, for the Lord your God goes with you; He will never leave you nor forsake you". How awesome is that? Once you are saved, He will mold you and shape you to the person you were meant to be.

It is very important that you learn to forgive others for the wrong they have done to you in order for God to forgive you of your sins. Why would God forgive you if you are not willing to forgive others first? Would you? Honestly?

When we ask God for forgiveness, He can forgive and forget. When He forgives us He wipes our slate clean. We as humans do not have that ability. Sure we can say we forgive someone until something comes up and reminds us of that offense again. Then all of a sudden we find ourselves mad at that person all over. When that happens we tend to let not only that event but all of them become a chain reaction where we bring up all the offenses that person has brought against us from the past. When we do that we are back to not forgiving them. This is how the devil works in us. Matthew 18:21-

22. Then Peter came and said to Him, "Lord, how often shall my brother sin against me and I forgive him? "Up to seven times". Jesus said to him, "I do not say to you, up to seven times, but up to seventy times seven". If you do not understand that completely. It is the same as God saying you need to give eternal forgiveness, basically over and over again.

You have to program your mind that when you choose to let something go and forgive that person, you are also choosing to forget it as well. Forgiveness or lack thereof can be a heavy burden. It can make you a very ugly person. It can cause a lot of unnecessary stress. Some people believe that forgiveness is the number one hindrance that stops God from hearing your prayer request or showing His will for you in your life.

I had to learn this the hard way. As you know, I had a lot of anger in my heart. It took me a long time to fight this. I can assure you when I did, I never felt better. I am happier, more pleasant to be around, I laugh more and I hope that I spread more joy to others. It is truly a disease if you do not take care of it.

Imagine every time someone offended you and you were not willing to forgive them. Because of that, you had to place a potato in a bag and carry it with you everywhere you went. Over a period of time, that bag would get extremely heavy. Unless you forgive those and let go of that extra burden. You can become completely miserable. Trust me; you will feel so much better when you do. People wrong us all the time. Can you imagine how many people do it unknowingly?

As a Christian growing in your walk with the Lord, you will learn how the Holy Spirit convicts you of your transgressions. Your conscience starts to eat at you. You know you did wrong. The devil knows that you did wrong as well. You feel bad, you ask God for forgiveness and He grants you that. Then the next thing you know, the devil is playing mind games with you so much that you end up not forgiving yourself. Don't beat yourself up over this. When you sin, confess, repent, and trust that the Lord has forgiven you and move on. Tomorrow is another day.

Confessing your sins can make you feel so much better, but remember forgiveness is not a license to sin.

Simply put, you can't go into a situation knowing you are going to sin, and say "Oh well, it's alright I will just ask God to forgive me". That is not how it works.

What you need to do is repent. Repenting is knowing that you sinned and are going to try to do everything in your power not to repeat that offense. This can be easier said than done, especially if you have developed a certain sin habit. You will probably sin, feel bad, then before you know it, you will sin again. Do not be discouraged, you have to work this out of your system. Some sin habits may be easier to break than others, such as drinking or cussing. Others may be more difficult such as lust, looking at women in a certain way, or gossiping. Just stay the course. I promise you will come out victorious.

I will say this over and over again because it is very important; the devil will do anything and everything to steal your joy and destroy your relationship with the Lord. You have to know this. He is the great deceiver and the master of lies.

You have to understand something that took me quite a long time to learn. Sinning or rejecting God's law separates you from having a healthy relationship with Him and can keep you away from His good graces. You have to understand that we are all born sinners. It is our human nature. What I struggled with was I would try very hard every day to not swear, control my temper, and everything else, which was not Christ-like. Of course, I would stumble.

When that happened, I felt or thought that God would never truly accept me because I had flaws. It wasn't so much that I made mistakes. We all do. I had the willingness to acknowledge my mistakes but asking for forgiveness was something else. What I had to understand was this was a transitional period. Even though I am not perfect, I tried to be. When I messed up I felt like God wouldn't forgive me, because I supposedly knew better. As I grew in my Christian life, I learned that God is very forgiving. I, on the other hand, was not as willing to forgive myself. When I asked for forgiveness, I vowed to try to do better the next time. What it comes down to is it is what is in your heart that God is after. Can you see my frustration with this?

Here are two instances where I chose to forgive someone. The first one that I want to mention was when I had been robbed. I had been a Christian for about a year at the time. I was working at a retail store and it was closing time. As we were shutting everything down, a customer came in and was looking for a particular item that we didn't carry. He continued to browse around the store and I went back to the counter area to finish my closing procedures.

The customer came up to the counter to use the phone. He said he needed to call his girlfriend because we didn't have what he was looking for. He grabbed the receiver of the phone with one hand and reached into his pocket with the other. When he pulled his hand out of his pocket, he was holding a gun. He demanded money. Thankfully, by that time our bookkeeper had already cleaned out the register with everything but the loose change. So, we gave him what we had on us. All I had in my wallet was $43.00. But it wasn't your average bills. They were bills that were dated between 1904 and 1920. I had brought them to work that day to take to the bank during lunch to see if they had more than face value, they didn't.

After he got our money, he made us get on the floor and count to 100. He didn't touch anybody nor did he point the gun directly at anyone. After he left, we called the police and our store manager. I had the next day off and it was a good thing as you can imagine I did not get much sleep that night. My manager who is also a Christian was concerned with my state of mind. He called me and asked how I was doing. I assured him I was alright, a little shaken, but fine. As I said, I couldn't sleep much that night. All I could do was keep running the events over and over in my mind.

Thinking how close I was to becoming a fatality. Then it hit me, I had to forgive the robber no matter what. Surprisingly it came easy. I forgave him so much that I went as far as to write a letter to the prosecuting attorney's office asking them to go easy on him.

They caught the suspect within a week. When he went to trial I attended the proceedings. His attorney had a copy of my letter, which she read to the judge before his sentencing. I am not sure how that weighed on the judge's decision, but he sentenced him to twelve years. During the trial, I noticed a couple of women who looked like they were family members. I approached them afterward and told them that I was a victim. I also told them I would pray for him. They hugged me and thanked me.

There was another time where I had to forgive someone that was not quite as easy. After my daughter and her mother had left. As you know I had become obsessed with trying to find them. My quest led me to the county courthouse. While I was there, I went to the Department of Health to obtain my daughter's birth certificate. When doing so, a notion came across that I should get a copy of my own as well.

As it turned out my birth certificate said that my last name was not the same last name that I had been living with my entire life. It had me listed with my mother's maiden name and no father at all. I took it home and compared it to the one that I had on file. The old birth certificate was nothing more than a fake; it said that I had a father. The same man that I thought to believe was my dad. After examining the two documents, you could see that there was some forgery involved. You can only envision what my reaction was.

I went to confront my mother about what I had discovered. You can imagine how many questions I had. I left her feeling that she was not honest with me. Because of that, I had more questions. Who was this man who had mistreated me all these years? Is that why he did all of those things to me? Who was my real father? Why would my mother not be truthful with me? What was her motivation in doing such a thing? My emotions ran wild. I couldn't help but speculate why no one loves me. I was a man without a family. My entire life has been one big lie. How was this going to affect the rest of my life? Was I going to have to get my name changed? How am I going to explain this? It is these types of situations that you need to reach deep down. I had been mad at a lot of people in my life, but I was really mad at my mother. I surely wanted to pay back the man who abused me throughout my childhood. I wanted it as bad as I ever wanted anything in my life.

I searched for answers with his family and my efforts got me nowhere. While I was probing, I found out that he moved out of state and couldn't be reached as he had no phone. So I was told. If I did find him. How was I to know he would be honest with me? I wanted to make a trip to where he lived. I wish I had because he died within a year. I did go to his funeral, but not to pay respects. I went with a motive to find the truth. Again, I got nowhere.

It took me years of grieving and feeling sorry for myself before I realized that I had to forgive my mother. It was through church and friends that I developed that desire to forgive. The fact that I didn't know who my real father was made it hard.

Then I realized I have a father, a father who loves me very much and will be there for me no matter what. That is God Almighty.

That is why it is important to develop a fellowship. Fellowship is having friends within your church community. It is having someone to call upon when you are struggling with a certain problem.

Fellowship is having people that can pray for you as well as you pray for them. It is someone that can help keep you accountable and to ensure you are spending time every day doing what you are supposed to do. I believe that fellowship or Christian friends are far more superior to your garden variety friend. These are people who genuinely care for you. I have developed some amazing fellowship relations over the years. So much so, that I do not miss what I had in the past. I haven't suffered one thing. I still enjoy my sports and have played in several golf tournaments. Do you know that contrary to what most people think, you can play eighteen holes of golf without drinking a single beer or cussing once and still have a great time? You can actually play better.

Fellowship is also described as the body of Christ. We all have our roles and together we function to do God's work. You have your pastor and your choir members. You have the piano and/or organ players. You have Sunday school teachers and nursery providers. You have a governing body such as treasurer and deacons as well as you have those who collect the offerings. We all serve a role in the body of Christ. We have those that are good speakers and motivators. We also have those that are good listeners. We are all given a special gift to assist with the body of Christ. You do not have to have a role in a church to be part of the body of Christ. We all have our special talents to do things outside of a church.

Think of the body of Christ as a lawn. All the blades of grass are the Christians. The weeds are sin. The lawn gets nourished by fertilizer, which is the word of God. It gets watered by the Holy Spirit. Then receives light from the sun, which is Jesus. The three of them work together and nourish the lawn which grows stronger and stronger and chokes out the weeds. When you mow the lawn you could say that it is like a revival, renewing it all over again.

Fellowship is the same as friendship. If you know anything about friendship it is not only having friends there when you need them but being there when your friends need you as well. It is surrounding yourself with good people. Think open-minded about your old friends that were not necessarily good for you. Take a close look at them. Would they be saying nice things to encourage you or would they be laughing at you? True friends will encourage you and try not to lead you down a path of destruction. Acquaintances are not true friends and could care less about you. Find new friends within the church community. You can have much more fun going to the movies, bowling alley, enjoying a ballgame or a round of golf than you will going to the bars and nightclubs.

I bet there are going to be times during this change when you are going to feel lonely. Don't fret; remember God is with you. He will reward you for suffering, by doing what is right. You could also use this change in your life to encourage your friends to follow you.

When I started making this adjustment in my life, I did get laughed at. But, my true friends were like my friend who is a Christian and supported me in my change. That friend, I am proud to call my wife, though we were not married at the time, she was a huge supporter. We spent several hours on the phone about my new life and the experiences I was going through. We talked about everything that was happening to me. Along with all the wonderful sensations, I was feeling. We discussed what

I was learning in the Bible, from church, and from the shows I watched on television. It was a very exciting time in my life. I will never forget it.

My family also supported me. My testimony was so strong when I discussed it with my brother. God worked through me to him and he started attending church. Not only did he attend, but he also volunteered to cut the grass.

Why does God give us free will? Freewill is the ability to love God, willingly without force. It wouldn't be very rewarding if we were forced to love Him. Have you ever been in or know of a relationship where one of the parties wanted to make the other one love them? It didn't work out, did it? That is the same way God works. If He forced us to love Him, it would not be a free will loving relationship nor would it be very effective. We also have free will when it comes to obeying His laws, just like the laws of society which are mostly Bible-based. We obey and love

Him with our free will, which means we do it because we want to. This is why the Bible is so powerful it tells how God knows us so well. He made us therefore he understands how we operate.

Chapter 9

Spiritual Warfare

Does God really exist?

This single question is probably the most asked in the world. It is asked because of one thing and one thing only and that is spiritual welfare. There are many forms of spiritual warfare and I will try to help you understand exactly what it is.

There have been scientists for many years that have had theories denouncing God's existence. The keyword here is "theory" and not proof. On the other hand, some scientists and archaeologists have discovered artifacts that can prove God's existence. For instance, there is the discovery of the Dead Sea scrolls. These scrolls have great historical and religious significance.

There is more than that. Take a look at God's existence on a larger scale. I am not a scientist but how would you explain the universe as a whole? Here, we have nine planets and some with moons suspended in mid-air orbiting the sun. How do you think that is possible without a higher being?

Scientists have tried to debunk the existence of God through the big bang theory. As late as 2011 NASA through the Hubble telescope, has made discoveries that can confirm what the book of Genesis has said all along. Remember earlier when I said that I had a hard time believing God's existence or the Bible? I believed that during the earlier years of mankind they were naïve and gullible because they had not experienced enough through time. This proves that I was wrong.

Now, look at the planet Earth itself geographically. On this planet, we have mountains, deserts, rainforests, oceans, rivers, and ice regions. If you take a step back and just look at these areas, they all are unique and beautiful in their way and they all serve a purpose.

If we were to break things down from there and look at all the different animals there are, it is truly amazing. We have over ten thousand different breeds of birdlife. There are over one hundred twenty-two thousand different species of marine life. As well there are over twenty thousand different types of animal life. There are some that believe that man may never know exactly how many different types of species there are throughout the entire world in all forms of life. How do you suppose all these came about?

Plantlife is also very fascinating. There is such a wide range of different plants. These plants all have a purpose ranging from being a food source to providing medicine to heal us from sickness or disease. You can see here that God has provided us with what all we need. Genesis 1:29; Then God said, "I give you every seed-bearing plant on the face of the whole Earth and every tree that has fruit with seed in it". They will be yours for food".

If we have all of these species, then explain to me where they came from? Some scientists or theorists will argue that man evolved from ape. Where did ape evolve from? What did a giraffe, elephant, or rhinoceros evolve from? What about the ostrich or hummingbird? How is it that birds can fly? Do you see my point?

Animals have their own unique defense systems as well you will find that certain animals live in unique parts of the world.

Scientists want you to believe that these animals have adapted to their environment. Really? How about this, God made each of these animals to survive in certain areas of the Earth. Could you imagine how long a scorpion could live in the arctic or a polar bear in the desert?

The theorists believe man evolved from ape because they are similar in appearance. This takes you back to the age-old question. What came first, the chicken or the egg? Theorists use this example because of one thing only, they do not believe in God. Could it be that Satan is working through them to create controversy?

We can also consider looking at the weather. We have everything from rain or snow to hurricanes and tornadoes. How is that possible? What purpose does the weather serve? Why is there no weather on the moon? Could it be because there is no life on the moon and there for no reason for weather or seasons?

Human beings are one of God's greatest creations. We have a variety of different races from Asian to African and Caucasian to Indian. He has given us so much within the confines of our bodies. We can see, hear, smell, taste, and feel. We also have the ability to express emotions such as love, hatred, laughter, and sadness to name a few.

God also gave us brains. We can think and function. We, through God, have technology so we can build a wide range of products from simple handheld radios to space ships to explore the universe. Don't forget the doctors that are able to cure us of life-threatening diseases and injuries.

The human body has organs that all have their own function. Livers, kidneys, and the digestive system. They all work together like a well-oiled machine. Yet, theorists want you to believe that all of this came from a form of bacteria.

Our bodies do not stop there. If we ponder the body and all its functions, we have legs to walk, arms to reach

and hands to grab. We have natural healing abilities. If
we cut our finger, in a couple of days depending on the
severity of the cut, it can be healed all by itself. In the
past couple of decades, scientists have discovered
DNA, which is a blueprint of genes in each and
everyone one of us. No two people are alike.

How can you explain all of this, except to say there is
a higher being? A higher being that has the wisdom that
we cannot comprehend. If there is such a higher being,
then you have a god.

Back to the question. Does God truly exist? Of
course, He does. Because there are scientists and other
agnostics for whatever reason or another do not want
you to believe He does. There you have spiritual
warfare. This battle has been going on since the
beginning of man. It affects us all in some case or
another without us even knowing it. It is everywhere
you look if you look hard enough.

That is where the Holy Bible steps in. The Bible, as I
said earlier, is considered a history book. It tells that
God created the Heavens and Earth and then instructed

mankind on how to function. If you read the books of the Old Testament, you cannot dispute the integrity. Many events have such great detail, too many details for someone to falsify. Do you know that no other religion or their god can make this claim?   Other gods are man-made. How do you create your own god to worship?

You did not live during the Revolutionary War, yet you believed it because you were taught it in school. If you can believe that piece of history then why would you not believe the history of the Old Testament? Does it not make sense that the Old Testament speaks a lot of God's existence as He directed His people on how to live, especially in the beginning of mankind? He had to be there or they may have been the cause of their demise. To think that man evolved from apes is ridiculous. If that is the case, then why do we still have apes?

Satan will use everything at his disposal to try to get people to dispute the existence of God. Science, archaeologists, your neighbor, your family, friends, television, radio, the internet, and whatever source he finds suitable.

Why do more people believe that the Revolutionary War took place than believe that God exists? That is because Satan has been very busy. He is the master of deceit and lies. He will do anything and everything to prove that God does not exist. He wants the worship, instead of us worshiping our Lord and Savior. Remember, it was his pride that got him kicked out of Heaven.

You would be wise to believe He does exist. When you do, you will see things on a grander scale. You will understand God's instructions and His purpose for us in our lives. Do you know one of the hardest degrees that there is to earn is in theology? The way I look at it is if you have enough intelligence to earn this degree, then you have enough intelligence to know whether or not God truly exists.

Some people want to believe only if they can see miracles. Open up your eyes and look around you. God is performing miracles every day. You may be saying to yourself, how or where because you do not see miracles such as the parting of the Red Sea. God is a solemn

God in which He is not going to get on a blow horn or put up a huge billboard saying, "Look at me, this is what I did today." He is not like the enemy who likes a grand stage to perform on. He doesn't need to. Look at what he has created already. He is performing miracles such as healing someone from a disease or answering prayers. He performs miracles that to some may seem small or quaint but let me assure you they have a higher purpose. He is also protecting you every day whether you realize it or not. Each day that you live to see the next, now that is a miracle. One of his biggest miracles is when you accept Him into your life. He exists because you have faith that He exists. Remember, faith is believing without seeing. Just like the Revolutionary War. Faith is knowing that miracles do happen. But then again, you can see these miracles if you just look close enough. My headache can be viewed as a miracle. It brought me closer to God.

Because I wasn't raised as a believer, I had no faith in God. That is exactly where the devil wanted me. I was already under his spell. But it was through God's love for me where He sent messengers or Angels to rescue me that I finally saw the light. Do you think that the gentleman I met at the gym or the nurse while I was in jail was accidental or coincidental? Do you want to talk about miracles? There is a miracle for you, my salvation.

It is easy for non-Christians to believe He doesn't exist because the devil is already in their lives and their heads. It was hard for me to believe God existed at first because I was trying to relate His existence with His goodness and love. How could He love me? After all, I was a deviant. But I did believe in the devil. Do not get me wrong, I did not nor have I ever worshiped him. I just had an easier time believing that Satan existed more than God. I saw more cruelty and harm in my life than I saw kindness and love. When I realized that for everything bad there was something good, it made it a little easier to see God's existence. Another reason why I didn't believe or know God because I didn't take the time to know Him.

Spiritual warfare is the constant battle between God and the devil over our souls. This battle is intense and it is everywhere. The more you know God's word, the more you will understand and see. There is one battle zone that you need to be aware of. That is in your head.

You will if you haven't already heard of the phrase "battlefield of the mind". What this means is, Satan will bring insecure or false thoughts into your head. He will do this in hopes that you will lose faith in God. If you don't have faith in Him, you will stop praying, worshipping, and telling others about Him. Now, on the other hand, God doesn't do this. God chose you; because He loves you and wants what is best for you. The devil could care less. Again, remember God gives us free will. Satan gives us temptation. God doesn't force us to love Him or believe in Him. If you belong to things of this world, you are on the side of the devil. If you ask God for help, He is just to give it to you as long as you make a commitment to be one of his followers.

Because God does give you free will, it doesn't mean that He doesn't love you. Nothing can be further from the truth. He is not going to force you to love him. That never works. However, He will send you signs that you are on a path of destruction; a wake up call if you will. For me, it was being arrested. His warning signs can be subtle enough, that you may not realize that there is a battle going on between Him and Satan over you. Nor do you realize how intense it is. Unless He has to, He's not going to give you an enormous alarm. Satan, since he is losing you will make all sorts of noise to keep you from following God. After you are alerted to these calls from God and you realize that you need to change your life around, you join his team. When you do this, the devil works harder than ever to get you back and the battle truly begins. Except now you are more aware of it.

When you ask God to come into your life, it is best if you give him complete submission. By doing this, you can help control the amount of spiritual warfare that you may encounter. Take the word of God and use it as food for your soul, nourish on it, dwell in it. Your salvation can be almost instantaneous; however, the transformation could take a while. Just like all of us are different, so will this journey.

By staying in the word of God, you will keep refreshing your mind of what is right and wrong. You will notice the signs more clearly when the devil is on the prowl and looking to attack you. Better yet, you will be able to defend yourself against him.

When I first got saved, I dove into God's word like it was the fountain of youth. After all, it truly is. When you soak it in, you feel rejuvenated and alive, like never before. I mentioned earlier you will have so much more peace within you. The feeling is truly indescribable. As I got into God's word, I was going to church on Sundays. I was attending Bible study on Wednesdays as long as my work schedule allowed it. I was reading the Bible every night for long periods. I was watching evangelists when I wasn't reading. I listened to the radio while I was sitting in my car eating lunch. I would glance over notes or listen to tapes of the services from my church over and over again. I was involved with complete submission to the Lord.

I really can't tell you how long that went on. I wish I could say it lasted, however it didn't. Somewhere down the line, a little at a time I started to get away from all I was doing, to the point where I wasn't doing hardly anything at all. I guess you can say I was getting too comfortable with everything and started to let my guard down. I still attended church but not regularly. I would go for a few weeks in a row and then take a week or two off. I stopped reading the Bible every day. I started watching my old programs and movies that weren't exactly Holy. I would watch gruesome murder movies or horror films or comedy that would not be suitable. Then, the next thing you know, I am going back to the bars and buying beer or alcohol. Before you knew it, I would start cussing more frequently as well as getting caught up in the rumor mill and everything else.

The reason why I mentioned watching television is very important. Because of that, I know some Christians that do not have tv's in their home. There are so many things out there that can pollute your mind. With all the junk on television nowadays it is almost impossible to avoid them. Television in itself is not bad, there are some wholesome programs out there. You should be selective about what you watch. For instance, if you watch a movie that has a lot of cussing in it, it could cause you to fall back and start swearing yourself. You could be lured into drinking by the beer commercials. At one time just like all other products being sold today, cigarettes had a big ad campaign. When was the last time you saw an ad in a magazine or a commercial for cigarettes? They have been banned. They seriously need to do that with some other products. Stay away from the programming that may have an impact on your life. At first, it may seem harmless, just like smoking, but before you know it, it affects you. Be careful of what you do in everything you do. Doing so you are showing God you are giving Him complete submission.

If you allow your mind to be polluted with garbage, it will produce garbage. All you need is something to spark impure thoughts. Then the battle of the mind truly begins. Maybe, a situation may occur that can cause you to have bad thoughts. Those thoughts can have an impact on you to act in an unholy way. Just like a simple little sin of lying can lead to something more serious.

I noticed the weeks that I did not go to church or wasn't as active in my Bible studies, things seemed to not go in my favor. It wasn't like things were horrible but they weren't zealous either. What usually followed were those pesky little temptations started to fill my head. Before you know it, I did what most people do. I fell back to my old ways. Occasionally I would get angry with God to the point where I started to blame him for everything that was wrong with my life. Going back to my

childhood, I questioned his love for me and told him I
was not happy with him and so forth.

The truth be known, I was the one to blame. God had
nothing to do with it. He did nothing wrong, it was me.
He will never change, rightly so, He is the same
yesterday, today and tomorrow. He is the creator not us.
It is us through the free will that we need to accept Him
and live the life he chooses us to live. We need to
change and stay on the course he has set for us.

Here is some food for thought. When you were a
slave to the world, the warfare was not as noticeable,
right? Did you ever take into consideration all of the
good days you had, even though you were not a
Christian? That could have been God working in your
favor. Then again, it could have been Satan tricking
you. That is why it is so important for you to know the
difference. God blesses you because He loves you.
Satan will use goodwill to leer you into a bigger trap.
Trust me on this. That is why you need to understand
God and how he works. As well as you need to know
your enemy. He knows you and what makes you tick.
There are a lot of people out there, Christians and non

that are so quick to blame God and don't ever consider giving Him his glory and thanking Him for all the good he has done.

I mentioned before I am a huge fan of Nebraska football. The 2002 season was not particularly a good season for them. They went 7-7 for the year. If you know anything about Husker football, that is not acceptable. During that season, on the nights that they lost, I got liquored up and called the defensive coordinator and cussed him up a storm. I asked him if he knew anything about defense, when and when not to blitz; or when to go with a nickel or dime package. Everything I could think of I was yelling at him.

His name was Craig Bohl. He put up with a lot of unnecessary junk from me and yet always remained calm and professional. Because of what I did, I would like to offer him a formal apology. There was no reason; despite my love for the team did he deserve the treatment he received from me. I judged him unfairly, I abused him with my tongue, and I got angry because of the losses. What happened here was I allowed the devil to attack me and take away my peace with the Lord. He used his tools and my weaknesses at his disposal to attack me.

Coach Craig has since moved on to head coach at the University of North Dakota State football team. He has done such a great job, that his team won three consecutive national championships. Way to go Craig.

One night I was very drunk and when I had called the university to reach Craig, I hit the wrong option on the phone system. Instead of getting Coach Bohl, I got Coach Ron Brown, who was the wide receiver coach at the time. I went on to stress my disliking of the team's efforts that day and the coaches needed to get tougher with the team. He listened for a while. Then he asked me if it was okay for him to speak. I agreed. Boy, did he let me have it, nicely, but still. He told me he was very happy that I was so passionate about the football team. But I need to be just as passionate for the Lord. He was hard, but kind if you can understand that. He went on to tell me that there was more to life than Nebraska football. Football may not last forever, but Jesus will. He put things into perspective for me that night. It was exactly what I needed to hear and for that, I dearly thanked him.

I went on to have two more encounters with Coach Brown after that. Once I ran into him at a shopping mall and he gave me an autograph. It wasn't just an autograph. He also wrote "Jesus loves you" and scribed Acts 20:24 which reads "But I don't care what happens to me, as long as I finish the work the Lord Jesus gave me to do. That work is to tell the good news about God's great kindness".

The other encounter was after he left the team, he went to work for the Fellowship of Christian Athletes based in Lincoln Nebraska. He also spoke at a local church and his messages were aired on a local television station on Friday nights. I watched him a couple of times and got this desire to talk to him more about God. One question I had for him. Was how did he receive such a passion and maintain it? So I called his workplace and left a message for him. I was fortunate enough that he returned my call and agreed to meet with me. We had a wonderful talk that day. I think it was close to two hours. He talked to me about his passion for Christ. How to place God first in everything you do and to just stay the course. He is a wonderful man and I don't think I can thank him enough. We parted with him giving me a business card in which he wrote down his cell phone number, in case I ever needed to call him again.

Because of the battlefield of the mind, it took me a while to get back on course, but the important thing was I did. It was shortly after that visit with Coach Brown when I felt God speak to my heart to write this book. I'll never forget that morning,

it was on a Friday that I woke up earlier than normal. Roughly an hour to an hour and a half which was unusual for me as I tended to sleep into the latest possible minute. Especially on Fridays knowing what kind of busy day I was going to have. Anyway, I woke up that morning with this wonderful idea racing through my mind, my heart was pumping and I was very excited. So, excited I had to tell someone. Who else would I call, but my best friend and later to become my wife. Before I went to work, I started making notes on what I wanted to write.

I started the book that night. It was all I could think about. I was working for God. I had a purpose and driven as ever. I kept it going for a while but unfortunately, that faded off. It wasn't that I gave up on the book. I think a lot of it was I had to reflect on what I was going to write about and make sure I cover everything I had learned.

Though I was excited to write the book I had to realize that I had to also grow in my relationship with God. I was still doing some of the same old things that were separating me from God. I had to get back to the basics. In some ways, it was harder than going through it the first time. I wish I could explain why or how but I can't. It is almost like a golfer who has a beautiful swing, then out of nowhere he loses it and has to re-invent it all over again.

One thing I would like to let you know is, even though you may have this great relationship with God. You will still have trials and tribulations. A trial is testing your faith and preparing you for the next level. Tribulation is a setback or a sign of oppression. It could be not getting a promotion or a series of setbacks. Either way going through these is God's way of building your relationship with him. He truly wants you to rely on him. When he comes through for you, you become so excited that you feel that you can't thank Him enough. When He doesn't give you what you ask for remember.

He may have something better in store for you, it's not the right time yet or He knows what is best for you in that particular situation.

When you are going through these times, you may think that there is no end and you cannot go through this any longer. Trust me, God will not give you more than you can handle. It is going to be tough to remember this. When you are going through these trials and tribulations, you really should be thanking God, because He is behind the scenes working on something in your favor. He is promoting you and I do not necessarily mean like a promotion at work so much as He could be promoting you to the next level in your faith.

Remember the story from earlier, when I dearly wanted the promotion at work and didn't get it. Now, this just goes to show you, how God will say "No", to prayer and give you something better. I think a lot of this was due to the fact, even though I went through a tribulation I did not make a scene or let it bring me down. Sure I was disappointed, it is our human nature. But it was how I handled it that made the difference. I was better off going to Lincoln. Seven months after that I was promoted again, to run a higher volume store which I am almost certain I wouldn't have received if I was promoted to the other store.

Reflecting on the scripture that coach Brown had given to me. Acts 20:24 it is our Christian duty to be servants of the Lord. Believe this or not, but as a servant to the Lord, we are to have our own ministry. Now that does not mean that we are all to be pastors of a church. But we are to plant seeds, tell others of the goodness of God's love. Remember what I said about the body of Christ being like a lawn. Well, that is the same here. Plant the seeds and let God through the Holy Spirit do his work. That is exactly what the gentleman at the gym and the jail nurse did. They spoke to me of God's love.

Going back to my Army days again, they told us that the Army would give back whatever we gave to it. This is very true with God as well. Give time to him, he will reward you. What I mean by this is. Some people say that they may not have time to go to church on Sundays. I beg to differ. I had said earlier on Sundays that I didn't go to church. It seemed like that week was more stressful than the times when I did go. On the opposite side, when I did go it seemed like I had more energy throughout the week as well as more things went my way. It seemed like I had more time to do the things I needed to or wanted to do. God will give you more than you give Him. He has me on several occasions. This doesn't necessarily mean, reading the Bible or attending church. It goes much further than that. Know this, no matter what you do or how well you do it. You will never out-give God.

I have heard several people tell me that they cannot spend time with God as much as they would like to. If you are willing to give God complete submission, then you are willing to give him time every day. How do you think you would feel if you got married to the love of your life? Then find out your spouse told you they didn't have time to spend with you daily. You would be upset after all they made a commitment to you on your wedding day.

Take the time to make an effort. Instead of sitting down and reading the newspaper which can pollute your mind or plopping down in your recliner to catch a game. Sit down, open the Bible, and just read. Or get up and go for a walk and just talk to God. Better yet, go to your neighbor's house and help him clean his gutters. We are creatures of habit so this may take some extra effort in the beginning. If you stay with it, it will become habit-forming and you will eventually do it without much thought.

Instead of your friends ridiculing you because you are willing to make a change, be a true friend to them and plant a seed. Tell them what you have learned and invite them to go to church with you. If they choose not to follow you, do not be discouraged, better they do that, than them steering you off course. Trust me the devil will sneakily use your friends to discourage you from your walk with God. That is where you need to rise above that and do what is right.

You are probably asking yourself by now. How can I have a ministry of my own? Or say "I do not have the ability to do such a thing". Nothing could be further from the truth. God gives us all special gifts to do his good work. Your gift or gifts could range from speaking, being a good leader, or just being quiet and living by example. You have more gifts than you know. Look deep inside yourself. What are you good at? What interests do you have? What things of this world make you sad? Take these things and use them to your advantage. Of course, there is always prayer. Ask God how he can use you.

One of my spiritual gifts is being able to reach out to others. Talk to them; say things that help them see the light. I have been able to get others to attend church with me or church functions such as Bible study. I have got them to go on their own. But remember it wasn't me, it was God working through me. My brother is a prime example. A couple of years after I accepted Jesus into my life, I had already moved to Lincoln so my brother came down to visit for the weekend. We went to watch the Nebraska baseball team play Boston College. After the game, we went to grab a bite to eat. During the game and mostly during dinner, I spoke to him about what the Lord was doing in my life. He took it to heart. The next thing I know he is attending a church close to his house in Omaha.

God gave me leadership skills. This has played out on several occasions. Being a leader is not always about being a boss or someone everybody has to answer to. Being a leader is much more than that, it is how you handle yourself in adverse situations. Have you ever watched a football game when a team commits a penalty and you may see their coach flipping out on the sidelines? How do you think his players perceive him? Maybe not so well. Then there's the coach, on the other sideline who remains calm. Sure, he may go out to contest the penalty to the referee, but he stays calm inside. What he is doing is showing his team that he is not going to let that one foul, disrupt his game plan. Staying focused, so his players will stay focused. Being a good leader can also be seen as motivating people to get them to do something they don't like to do or they feel they can't do.

There have been times, rather at work or other places, which I have learned to control my temper. I can't say I did it all the time but, compared to how I used to be. There has been an improvement. It is not me, however; it is God working through me. I made a commitment to Him in which I wanted to remove this from my life, and it is working.

So, when the devil tries to throw you a curveball to disrupt what good things you have going with the Lord, remain calm. Remember that God is on your side. Tell Satan that he is not going to ruin your day. You can tell him to leave you alone through the name of Jesus. As you grow in your faith, you will learn that Jesus gives you the authority to fight the devil yourself.

God also gave me a love for animals. Everyone who knows me knows how much I love animals, especially dogs. Dogs in my eyes are truly a gift from God. I believe God gave them souls and when they die, they do go to Heaven like the rest of us. How can you argue with that? A dog's love like God's is unconditional. It is our Christian duty to take care of them as well as all animals. Since I received the gift of my dear sweet dog

"Husker", my whole outlook on animals has changed. I have learned to appreciate them more, in such a way that I became a better provider and caregiver. I love animals so much that when I made trips to the mountains my trip would not be complete until I saw every type of animal that I was looking for that lived in that region.

Animals are truly one of God's blessings and it hurts me deep down inside when others hurt them. They are defenseless and cause no harm unless they are provoked. I have been known to say a little adage similar to the famous Will Rogers. 'I have never met a dog I didn't like". I truly believe that there is no such thing as a bad dog, just bad owners. Just like I don't think there are bad people, just bad influences.

God gave me a gift to show concern for my fellow man. I will always go to battle for a friend or colleague who needs help. I was born a fighter and always will be. However, I fight for God now. I fight the good fight. I consider myself to be a Christian soldier, fighting for the good of mankind. Standing up for the weak, not only that, but standing strong in my faith, and not wavering against God's word or His glory.

So, you see you may have several gifts that you may or may not know about. Take a step in faith, do not fret. God is on your side. He will not leave you nor forsake you. You just need to stay the course and keep Him first in everything you do.

God will strengthen you; you no longer have to live in fear. Remember he chose you. He got your attention. He wants you to live an abundant life. Now know this, abundance can mean being rich. But there are two different ways to be rich. You can be rich financially or rich spiritually. If he blesses you with wealth, good for you, it is possible. There are a lot of folks that are rich and yet don't have a relationship with the Lord. That wealth is worth nothing if you are not rich spiritually.

It is truly sad to know of someone who has all the money they do and do not have a relationship with God. Their riches here on Earth will do nothing for them in going to Heaven. When they die, more than likely their estate will be divided amongst their family, and then there is nothing after that. Their money, unfortunately, cannot buy them a ticket to Heaven. Think about this. When we die we all get buried in the same size coffin.

Do not live in fear. God will strengthen you. If you start off loving him for possibly the wrong reason like I did in the beginning. He will change your heart and mind. He will remove your stinking thinking. The next thing you know you will become a God-fearing Christian. Now being God-fearing does not mean that you fear Him like some stalker in the middle of the night or like I did my father. It means He has such an impact in your life, that you fear sinning and separating yourself away from Him and letting him down. His word has become so involved in your life that all you want to do is His good work.

One of the nicest compliments ever paid to me. I was at work, trying to explain to a woman why she needed a certain service. She asked me if I was being honest with her or just trying to make a sale. One of my employees who knew her through another acquaintance told her. "He isn't going to lie to you. He's a good Christian". I

never thought I would ever hear those words directed
towards me because of my previous lifestyle.

Chapter 10

Convenient Christians

I used to believe that I was an atheist. An atheist is someone who does not believe in God. But after learning of the word "agnostic", I realized that I wasn't an atheist after all. I was an agnostic. An agnostic believes that there is a higher being but unsure of what he or it may be.

If you have ever considered yourself to be one of the above or both, do not give up hope. You can still have a relationship with God. There have been many notable people throughout the ages that didn't believe God existed. When they discovered He did, He was not only able to turn their lives around spiritually, but He also went on to help them do great things. So, no matter what your circumstances, know that God can work through you to do many wonderful things. I am a living testimony to this. Do not ever think or feel that you do not deserve God's love and kindness.

I believe that convenient Christians or false prophets act like agnostics in a way. The reason why I say this is because of what I experienced in Christians before I became a believer. They did not do Christianity any favors by living double standards. The Bible warns you of these types of people. Rather it is through false prophets or convenient Christians.

In some ways you can consider the two to be one in the same. They both manipulate the word of God for their gratification. They believe that they can act and behave however they want and that God does not know their intentions or thoughts. Some of these people would even go so far to say that God doesn't know everything you do, especially behind closed doors.

Some scriptures warn of these false prophecies. Deuteronomy 18:20-21; But the prophet who presumes to speak a word in my name that I have not commanded to speak, or who speaks in the name of other gods, that same prophet shall die. And if you say in your heart, "How may he know the word that the Lord has not spoken".

Jeremiah 14:14; Then the Lord said to me, "The prophets are prophesying in my name. I have not sent them or appointed or spoken to them. They are prophesying to you false visions, divinations, idolatries and delusions of their minds.

Matthew 24:24; For false messiahs and false prophets will appear and perform great signs and wonders to deceive, if possible, even the elect.

Psalm 139 tells you that God knows everything about you.

These were the type of people that turned me away from really wanting to have a relationship with the Lord. When I was younger, I saw what they said or heard what they believed and it just didn't add up. So, it kept me away.

The devil will attack all of us at different times throughout our lives. Just because you are a Christian doesn't necessarily mean that you are exempt. Again going back to spiritual warfare, hard core Christians should know this and hopefully identify it but, they don't always. I am warning you about becoming a convenient Christian and to be sympathetic and helpful of the ones you may encounter as well as to stay clear of false prophets.

These false prophets can have a negative influence on your spiritual growth. They know the Bible as well as any other. But their actions in living a Holy life beg to differ. I always wondered about those pastors who have such a miraculous healing touch. Yet it is these same pastors that make people spend a lot of money to get healed. If Jesus were here today, He would not be asking for money to heal them. Instead he would be traveling from hospital to hospital healing all those who are sick. It is pastors like this that can give Christianity a bad name.

There are also those pastors that claim to be prophets and start cults. Cults are very dangerous and, in some cases fatal. These prophets or pastors have such power over their followers through brain washing or manipulation that they have cost followers their lives. David Koresch and Jim Jones are probably the more notorious of these types. You have to be careful, they are out there and I suggest choosing wisely. Get involved with a church through some association with another person. A church that has been in existence for a long time and that is Bible based.

There are indicators that you can use to verify if the organization you belong to is a cult. One of them is that the leader of the group chooses to be worshiped instead of God. They also try to manipulate your lives by telling you where you can work, live or where your kids can attend school. They can go so far as to tell you who you can marry, if at all. They will try to recruit you, usually when you are at a low period in your life. They will also come down on you if you say anything negative against them or their leader. Be very careful that you do not fall into this trap. False prophets in my opinion are working for the devil and using God's word for their gain.

There are four ways to look at convenient Christians. The first way is someone who thinks that just because they go to church, that they can behave however they want during the rest of the week. They manipulate the Bible mainly by translating what it means for them to behave in a particular manner. Joyce Meyers has a wonderful saying that I like to use a lot. "Just because you sit in a garage, that doesn't make you a car". Very true.

For instance, the Great commission which is Matthew 28:18-20. Jesus came to them and said: "I have been given all authority in Heaven and on Earth! Go to the people of all nations and make them my disciples. Baptize them in the name of the Father, the Son and the Holy Spirit and teach them to do everything I have told you. I will be with you always even until the end of the world".

What Jesus was saying was that we need to be active as Christians. We need to get out and tell others about Him. We can't just go to church on Sunday and be inactive the rest of the week. Remember when I said we are to have our own ministry. There you go.

Secondly, convenient Christians have a "Do as I say, not as I do' mentality Let's look at this in the form of forgiveness. It would be wrong for you to instruct someone to forgive another when they were wronged and then in turn when you are wronged, you decide not to forgive. Matthew 5:39 Jesus says "But I tell you not to try to get even with a person who has done something to you. When one slaps your right cheek, turn and let him slap the other cheek". Besides, how wrong is it to ask God to forgive you when you sinned against Him, yet you won't forgive your neighbor.

A third type of convenient Christians is referred to as "sally port Christians". These are people who only want to believe in God as long as they are in a particular situation like sitting in a jail cell. These are the types of people who vow to change their ways for God to help them in certain situations. Once He does, they go back almost immediately to their old, evil ways again. There have been many celebrities who have gone to jail and said that they received God while they were incarcerated. Shortly after they are released, they are seen at a Hollywood night club in a drunken stupor. That is using God. I would be very careful in a situation like that.

Don't get me wrong, I am neither passing judgment on these people nor criticizing them. First of all, I can remember when I accepted the Lord into my life. I had some obstacles to overcome and things to learn as well. I know it can be very difficult. But don't use God to gain instant satisfaction then throw Him to the curb like yesterday's newspaper. That in my eyes is playing with fire.

The fourth way could also be someone who proclaims they know God but do not serve or worship Him. Christmas is the most celebrated holiday in the world. Yet, if you look at all those that celebrate Christmas and then compare that to those who attend church regularly. The numbers are staggering. At Christmas time, it seems everyone is believers. But where are they the rest of the year? What bothers me are all the people who go shopping for their families and friends to buy them nice gifts while knowing all along they too will receive
something in return. Their motive of giving is wrong. You should give for the pleasure of giving, not expecting to receive in return.

What is the true meaning of Christmas? Isn't it the celebration of the birth of Christ? Since we are to celebrate it, shouldn't we celebrate it correctly? There are so many people in this world that celebrate Christmas and yet they do not step foot into a church to offer Him praise. It's the "What's in it for me?" mentality that has me concerned about my fellow man and what sort of future they may be missing out on.

How many times have you seen or heard of people who rush to the store to get their child the hot new toy of the Christmas season. Suddenly two parents are fighting physically to grab the last one of that toy off the shelf? Do you think that either one of those two parents attend church? People have died in situations like this. Is this the way it should be? Do you think that is how Jesus would want us to behave or celebrate His birthday? There are so many people that want to celebrate Christmas, but do not want to celebrate its true reason for the season.

As wonderful as Christmas is, there is a holiday that is more deserving in my eyes, and that is Easter. There are even fewer people that celebrate Easter than Christmas. Easter is the celebration of Jesus' ultimate sacrifice. It is the basis of Christianity. Christmas would

be meaningless if there were no Easter. What Jesus did
that day on Calvary is more than anyone can imagine.
He became the sacrificial lamb where He was nailed on
the cross to die for all of our sins and strengthen the
communion between God and mankind. Every year
during the Easter season, I watch one or more movies
that depict this time of Jesus' life here on Earth. I do it
for my spiritual growth and
cleansing. To see what He did for all of us and to sit
back and look at all I am because of Him. It rejoices my
heart and renews my mind.

On Easter just a couple of years ago, my wife and I
had gone to church to celebrate. While on the way home
we drove by a particular retail store. The parking lot was
packed. I couldn't believe how many people were
shopping instead of spending their morning thanking
Jesus for what he has done for all of us.

What made me sad was when I thought about the
employees of that store. Working in the industry myself,
I know the pressure that bosses can put on employees
to work certain days of the year. I wondered how many
employees were not afforded the opportunity to attend

services that day as opposed to losing their jobs just because someone wanted to go shopping.

I said earlier that God gave me the vision to write this book and it took me a while to complete it. That Easter Sunday was the finalization that I needed to go through with it. So I began.

My thoughts went beyond that. How sad is it that corporate America has to make that almighty dollar at all costs? Is it enough where they have to open the doors on Sunday? If the CEO's of that company truly honored God's word to not work on Sunday. I trust that He would reward them even greater. This also makes me wonder how effective the enemy has been in the practices of Corporate America. He has a stronghold on them to where they think they need to be opened on Sundays. The enemy works hard to deceive all of us, not just personally but through many avenues.

From that point on, I vowed to never go to a business establishment on Sunday again. I feel if I do, then I am just encouraging the owners of these companies to stay open. The way I look at it is, if I didn't get it by Saturday it would have to wait until Monday. I took this matter even further by writing the editors of all the national newspapers encouraging believers to follow suit. I have no idea how many published my letter if any but, I was very passionate about this. When I think of all those who do not know God, it really hurts deep inside.

My heart goes out to those that are non-Christians. Over the years I have had several discussions with non-believers. The things they say or how they feel about God can in some ways, shock even me. I can only hope and pray that they get saved and see the wonders of God's love like I do. I contribute most of that to the fact that they have never been allowed to know God. Or if they did, they refused it for one reason or another. Was it the inconvenience of going to church or reading the Bible? Or was it they had some sort of negative influence from a friend or family member? There again, it's the enemy doing whatever he can to keep us separated from God. Satan has a stronghold on so many.

On my way to church every Sunday, I drive by homes of those that you can just tell are not out going to church. Their cars are parked in the driveway; you see them mowing their lawns, getting their boats ready or whatever. These are generally the same people that will celebrate Christmas and maybe Easter and to nothing else the rest of the year.

I have had people tell me they do not have the time to go to church. I beg to differ. If you go to church and spend time with God, He will reward you. He knows what you have to do throughout the week. If your heart is pure and you want to spend time with Him. He will help you do what you need to accomplish. He will afford you more time or energy to do what you need. I can speak very highly in this area. He is so awesome. You just have to believe in Him.

There is something to be said about non-Christians. I know several people that are and I have asked them about their feelings or thoughts about God. Some say they just do not want to be bothered. Others believe that religion is a hoax. Then some feel that churches ruin man's relationship with God. These people are not troublemakers. they are good everyday citizens. They just feel for one reason or another that it is not

necessary to have a relationship with God. Their lives
are normal; they have good spouses and nice jobs,
probably very loving families. They just do not know
God or have Him in their hearts. Could it be that they
have been negatively influenced by convenient
Christians? I think so. After all, they influenced me.

I guess you can say convenient Christians feel that
they don't need to make any improvements in their lives.
These people are only fooling themselves. Before I was
a Christian, I was always looking to improve myself. I
used to say that I learned from my mistakes and
because of that, I hoped to make a million of them.
Knowledge is power. When you have knowledge, you
have understanding which gives you power. James 1:5
says; "If any of you lack wisdom, you should ask God,
who gives generously to all without finding fault, and it
will be given to you". Isn't God awesome?

If convenient Christians knew God, then they wouldn't
be so quick to complain, criticize or blame Him for
everything wrong in their life. I could not believe how
much I used to do this. First of all, how can you blame
someone who is not involved in your everyday life? It

doesn't make sense. If you do not have Him in your life,
He is not going to help you out. You do not worship
Him, you do not obey Him and you are following the
ways of the world. You belong to the enemy. If you
choose to accept the Lord into your life, He will come
through in times of difficulty. Don't get me wrong, you
will have some setbacks. He is allowing these setbacks
so you can grow spiritually and you will be more
victorious than if he wasn't involved at all. He is
protecting you and will see you through every adverse
situation. Only He can turn tragedy into something
good. He has for me in so many ways. If He is not
involved, that same situation could end up being worse
for you.

Being a Christian is a very wonderful way of life.
There is however no such thing as a perfect Christian.
We are human and will make mistakes. God knows
this, He created us and knows more about us than we
do ourselves. When you take that first step in your
spiritual walk, remember this always. Just as you may
have a child that you are raising, they have to learn what
you are teaching them. You know they love you as
much as you love them. Yet, they are going to make

mistakes. Do you punish them harshly when you know that they were trying? I bet you love them unconditionally and correct them? This is how God will work in you and with you. As long as you are willing to improve yourself every day and look to God for direction and understanding, you will be just fine. Keep putting your best foot forward, you will never stop growing with God.

My Christian life has brought me through many stages. I pray that you will be aware of some of the obstacles that I have encountered and handle them better than I did. Just like we are all different in our DNA, so is our relationship with God. He treats us All the same, yet he treats us differently. That shows how amazing he truly is.

When I first started, I had no idea that I would end up having this strong desire to serve him in so many capacities. I look at the famous speech that President John F. Kennedy made on the day of his inauguration. "Ask not what your country can do for you, but what you can do for your country". That is the mentality that God has instilled into me. All I think about nowadays is

"What can I do for Him?" He has performed an amazing transformation in my life.

I have been very fortunate to get involved with a good church, where I have had the distinct honor of doing God's work. I helped remodel the kitchen at the church. I have hosted a small group study. Then I was asked to teach a small group study. You have no idea how excited I was when I had that opportunity. I felt like I had reached the next level of my walk with the Lord. Now I am writing this book. But it is just not those types of things. It is doing things all day long, everyday. It is your character and how you behave, people are watching. They are just not watching their noticing what is different about you and how you conduct yourself and the kindness that shows your true heart. I do not know what God has in store for me in the future, but I can hardly wait.

I attended a prayer breakfast some years ago. During that breakfast the chaplain from the county jail gave his testimony. I was very touched by this, so much that I contacted him a couple of days later. I told him that I too wanted to preach to those that were incarcerated. He invited me to his office. While I was there, I gave him a brief of my testimony and told him I wanted to serve. He thought it was a wonderful idea. But first, I had to pass a background check. I wasn't worried considering my past. I knew if God wanted me there, he would make it happen. It did. I volunteered for close to two years. I will never forget my first time. I gave a lengthier version of my testimony and afterwards, received a standing ovation. What a rush.

This brings me to another question of the ages. What is the meaning of life? The meaning of life is simply put in Deuteronomy 6:4-5. "Love thy God, your Lord with all your heart, soul and strength". How do you love God? First of all worship Him and give thanks for all you have regardless of how bad you feel your situation may be. Remember it could always be worse and regardless He will help see you through it. We can love Him by helping others and spreading the word.

I am truly thankful for a second chance in life. I cannot imagine what my life would be like right now without Him. I was not going in the right direction. I have grown in so many areas that I don't think I could count them all. God changed my life to where things that normally would have bothered me don't any longer. The things I used to get angry with, no longer faze me. The sins of the flesh that used to control my life, no longer do.

I cannot speak of all the things I have learned since I accepted God. All I can truly say is that he saved me from eternal damnation. He has shown me there is a better life out there and it is available to all who accept Him and believe in Him.

I pray that all who read this book come to learn what I have and hopefully more. That they look to the Lord, confess their sins and ask God for knowledge and guidance in their lives. That they do not get discouraged and always remember that God is with them especially when it doesn't feel like He is. I pray that you no longer remain stubborn and become open-minded and teachable.

Chapter 11

Being a Real Man

As I ponder over my early years in life and what God was doing through me, I noticed that He was teaching me what and what not to do as far as being a real man.

So, what does it take to be a real man? First of all, you have to come to the conclusion that you need and want improvement in your life. That you, like all of us, have flaws. Everyone in this world can use a little improvement. That being a real man is not conducting yourself in the ways that your past has taught you. Once you decide you need a change for the better, remember the following:

Being a real man is not how many beers or whiskey shots you can drink. When I used to drink on a daily basis, I thought I was tough by drinking. The truth is the only thing it did for me was make me more tolerant of alcohol which in turn caused me to spend more money to get drunk. What got me was how some guys thought they were so tough by staying up all night drinking, yet these were the same guys who weren't tough enough to get out of bed and report to work the next day because they had a hangover. Drinking yourself into a drunken stupor is not only unmanly, but it is also foolish as well.

Being a real man is not how many fights you can get into or how many people you can beat up. As I was growing in my relationship with the Lord, I became impressed when I would see guys that would get in some sort of disagreement. You could see that they were just steaming on the inside. You know they wanted to take a
swing at someone. Instead of getting stupid and throwing a tirade or starting to hit someone, they remained calm and talked their way through it. I was very impressed and wanted to be more like this.

I finally learned how to accomplish this. The first time I did it, I'm not going to lie, I thought I was a coward. Then I realized how much better the situation turned out since no one went to jail, especially me. I was pleasantly surprised when I realized how much more control I had and how others looked at me positively for staying calm

in the situation. I was maturing as a Christian and it was
an awesome feeling.

Each time you fight you are taking a chance. There is
always someone bigger, tougher, and meaner than you.
These days' people don't fight like the days when I grew
up. Today they use weapons of all kinds. Don't be stupid
like I was. I always thought if a guy had to take out a
gun or knife instead of beating me hand to hand, that I
was the bigger man in the long run. I may die, but he's
the true coward because he had to use a weapon. Even
today with all the fights I have been in, I cannot see
someone using a weapon on someone else. The only
weapon used on me was a set of brass knuckles and
that is nothing compared to today. But, the guy who
used them on me was thought of as a lesser man by
those that witnessed the fight.

Being a real man is not running off at the mouth and
swearing up a storm. Practice your intellect. Use wiser
words. Through this, you will show respect not only for
yourself but for others around you. I have always been
appalled whenever I saw someone who would cuss in

front of the elderly or a mother with her kids. Is it really necessary to cuss?

Stop hanging around the water cooler sitting in on the gossip or spreading gossip yourself. Even though you may not always spread the gossip, listening to it can be just as bad because you are encouraging it. You will gain respect from others if you walk away once these conversations startup. Being a real man is not telling stories to make yourself look bigger or meaner than you are.

Being a real man also means understanding that you may be a product of your environment so don't hang out with the wrong crowd. Don't let others influence you to make bad decisions. Be wise and make choices that are good for you and your family. So many young men have good hearts, yet they can be so easily influenced to do something stupid that may seem like fun, but ends up being wrong. The unfortunate thing is they get caught up with individuals who can lead them into trouble. It only takes a spark to start a fire.

Being a real man is not disrespecting women. Women are not statistics, nor are they to be looked down upon. It always bothered me when guys would label their girls by "old lady" or other inappropriate words that they use nowadays. Women are also not to be considered slaves. It is not their job to cook and clean while you sit around with the guys and drink beer. Be a real man and help your girl around the house, surprise her with a home-cooked meal once in a while and treat her with love and kindness. She is as much a child of God as you are. Another thing, would you appreciate a guy calling your daughter his "old lady", or mistreating her in any way? The problem is if your daughter sees you do that to her mother, she may feel that is acceptable.

It is pretty well known that when guys get sick, we can be the biggest babies around. Guess who is always there to take care of us? The women in our lives. Be appreciative that you have that special person in your life. Repay the favor when she is not feeling well.

Stay away from women that seem willing to have sex with you right away in your relationship with her. My experiences have taught me that these types of women are no good. They do not have morals or values. If they are that easy with you, they will be the same with others. I warn you about the sins of the flesh. Control yourself and do not deflower an innocent young lady as well. Show concern for her. Control your desires and show patience.

When it comes to marriage, there is no need to try to get married right away. Marriage is a bond for life. Make sure that it is exactly what you want to get into. One of the best ways to do this is to be pure. Avoid physical contact, which can flutter your judgment on whether or not she may be the one for you. Spend some significant time with her before you make a serious commitment.

When I was younger, I tried to help out my friends with their relationship problems. I've always felt that I had a knack for helping others. One thing I used to tell my friends was that in a relationship, only one of two things are going to happen. Either you will stay together forever or you won't. It's a fact of life. Marriage needs to be taken seriously. It is a union that God created for us. I think the reason the divorce rate is so high is couples may not have God in their lives. They rush to marriage and then rush to divorce. They take the easy way out instead of trying to work themselves through their problems.

Women are not to be punching bags. If you are married, this is the woman who may be now or later raising your children. What kind of example is it to teach your sons that it is okay to hit their spouse? What kind of message are you sending your daughter? What if she meets up with an abusive man? This is your defenseless daughter. Do you want some guy punching on her all the time? You could be sending out the wrong messages because she saw you beating your wife and she probably thinks that is the way real love is to be shown or given. Your sons will grow up to be like you and your daughters will marry men like you.

Being a real man is being kind and loving to your children. It is spending time with them each and every day. Giving them hugs and kisses, telling them you love them. Sitting down at night and spending quality time with them. Play a game or watch a wholesome movie. Help them with their homework, if needed. Give them confidence not only in love but with all things they may encounter as they grow.   Take time to be a part of their everyday lives. Go support them at their athletic events or school activities. If they make a mistake, be there to comfort them and don't ridicule or discipline them too harshly. One day you are going to be pretty old. You are going to need your children to help you out with many things. The love and kindness you give them as a child will be rewarded back to you when you need them the most.

Being a real man is not showing hatred towards others just because they are different. It still amazes me today, years after all the race riots and whatever else that was going on during the sixties, that there is still a huge amount of hatred directed to those who have a different skin color. I am very proud to say that even though I was the way I was, I did not have a prejudiced bone in my body. What was really sad is that I saw it in the Army. It's ridiculous to not like someone who could possibly save your life because he didn't look the same as you. Have you ever seen the movie "Crash"? How sad has this world become where there can be so much hatred?

Then there is the hatred towards homosexuality. There are many scriptures in the Bible that clearly state the act between two men or women is unholy. But, Jesus always said love the sinner, not the sin. They are just like everyone else in this world. Don't ridicule them. Pray for them. Do not get caught up in the ways of the world. It has gotten so bad that I never thought I would see the day when we would be using the term "Hate crimes" in our judicial system. Not just for homosexuals but race as well.

Hatred is not just with the opposite races or the gay community. It is toward anyone. It is time to have a change of heart If you find yourself showing hatred in your heart towards anyone for any reason, it is probably time to pray for God to work in you. Hatred is a disease, and like most diseases, it can be hereditary, but it can be cured. The reason why I say hereditary is I personally feel that we are taught to hate just like we are taught in other negative ways.

If your parents taught you wrong, don't beat them up because of it. They may have been taught wrong themselves. Pray that they receive God's knowledge as well as the blessing of the Holy Spirit. Remember we did not come to this world with an instruction manual or a warranty. There is only one instruction manual and that is the Holy Bible. If they did not know how to use that, do not fault them.

Stop being so sensitive to what others say to you or the names they call you. Who cares? I'm telling you, you'll be better off walking away from it, not seeking revenge, and better yet not dwelling on it. I have been called a lot of things in my life and not one of them hurt me   There is a saying that goes, "What others think of you is none of your business". Isn't that the truth? Whatever happened to the phrase, "Sticks and stones may break my bones, but names will never hurt me?"

Being a real man means being neighborly. Help your fellow man by showing how God can work through you and help others in time of need. Better yet, volunteer your services. Even if the person doesn't look needy, jump in, and help anyway.

Being a real man means to not be lazy in your affairs. If you have a list of things to do, get up and get going with them. It also means being responsible for your duties and not putting your workload onto others. The book of Proverbs highlights hard work, quite frequently. God does not award laziness.

Being a real man also means confessing all the wrongs you do. Do not try to cover it up. When you confess your sins, God will forgive you and you will feel better about yourself.

Being a real man means being a good provider for your family. So many relationships have problems due to finances. Be the man of the house. Do you need the little extras such as cable television or eating out at nice restaurants? Cut back on things that are not necessary and spend your money wisely. There is a big difference between needs and wants. Do not spend your money foolishly and take food or clothes away from your children. Your family is your responsibility.

There was a guy I worked with. Every day his wife would drive to our workplace to find out what he wanted for lunch. Then she would go get his lunch, drive back, eat, and then go home. The rest of us usually brought our lunch to work. They wasted money and gas doing this every day. When they received their income tax return, instead of doing something nice with the money like spending it on their kids. They bought a stereo system for their car and got matching tattoos. Seriously?

Being a real man means finding ways to forgive others. Life is too short and precious to go around holding grudges. It weighs heavy on your mind and your heart. It really drains you and causes unnecessary stress which could lead to other health problems. Learn to let it go. Do not seek revenge. Have you ever watched a football game when two players get into a little scuff? One player pushes or hits another, then the second one retaliates and he is the one the referee sees and gets a penalty thrown at him. Jesus said if someone strikes you on the cheek, turn the other way so he may strike the other one as well.

Being a real man is having a personal relationship with God. The Bible teaches that we as men are to be the spiritual leaders of the household. That goes much further than being the driving force to get your family up and going on Sunday mornings. It is through all your actions. Praying before you eat dinner and giving thanks for all you have. Remaining calm during adverse situations, being a solid rock for your family, and letting your light shine as a child of Christ. Love your family and others unconditionally. The family that prays together stays together.

Being a real man is being kind, sensitive, loving, caring, thoughtful, forgiving, patient, and understanding.

Being a real man is trying to do your best every day and conducting yourself as God wants and is teaching you to act.

Being a real man is acting just like Jesus. What would Jesus do? That is what being a real man is all about.

So what did Jesus do? First of all, He loved everyone. He reached out to everyone to show them the love that our Heavenly Father has for all of us. He showed everyone what a kind heart is capable of as opposed to a closed fist. He walked and gathered fishers of men, He healed the lame, made the blind see and the deaf hear. He even brought the dead back to life. He was questioned as to why he sought the sinners. His reply is priceless. Mark 2:15-17. "It is not the healthy that need a doctor, but the sick. I have come not to call the righteous, but the sinners".

You need to make a commitment, a pledge to read, and follow God's word. Start by reading the Bible every day. It doesn't matter where you start as long as you get started. Before you read, ask God for knowledge and understanding. He will give that to you unconditionally. I have found that you can read a particular scripture and it can have a particular meaning to what obstacle you are facing in your life. Then, later on, you could be facing a different obstacle and read the same passage and it can have a totally different meaning. That is how wonderful I have found the Holy Bible and God's word to be.

I started out reading the New Testament first. I found it to be easier to follow than the Old Testament. It is also the most recent events. Not only that, but the parables that Jesus tells of can be used as life lessons for us to apply every day.

As you read these parables and the life and times of Jesus, you will find out what an amazing man He was while He was in his ministry. Know this, he studied and prepared for thirty years for a three-year ministry. Being a man like Jesus is being a real man.

Next, you need to get involved with a Bible-based church. You may ask yourself, aren't all churches Bible-based? Sadly, no. A Bible-based church is one that reads scriptures during the service and will spend most of the sermon going into great detail with what that scripture says and means. It breaks it down in layman's terms so that you are able to understand it better and apply it to your life.

You also should get into a church that has a good foundation of fellowship. Fellowship is a gathering of people who in general have good hearts. People that invite you to church gatherings assist you in your spiritual growth and show genuine concern for you as a person. Believe it or not, I have been to churches that have had neither one or in some cases both. If you go to a church service and you find yourself wanting to go back, then you have found a good Bible-based church with good fellowship. Remember the church is not a building. It is a gathering of two or more people who worship the Lord and do his good work.

Earlier I said that you need to make a commitment. This is very true. But is also true in anything you want in life. I am an athlete. What do athletes do more than just play the game? They practice, they train and work hard for hours for the prize or the victory. The game or event is merely a test from all the training. Do you think that a person just wakes up one morning and decides to run a marathon? If so, what are his chances of winning or better yet finishing the race? I would say the odds are highly against him. A marathon runner has to train every day, no matter what the circumstances. There are days when he doesn't feel the greatest, had a bad day at work, or may have a full plate of other chores or errands he needs to do. Yet, he will find or make the time to train for that race. He will have to run for weeks or months to compete in a race that will only take a couple of hours.

Making a commitment to Jesus won't be as physically demanding as training for a marathon. But the victory will be much greater. To be victorious you need to practice every day. Practice by applying yourself to read the Bible. Take what you read, meditate on it, and apply it to your everyday way of life. There are so many scriptures that you can use. It's amazing. Get out of bed on Sundays and go to church. Learn to thank the Lord for all your blessings and praise Him always.

Joel Osteen has a favorite quote. He always says "Fight the good fight." I do this every day. God has instilled in me that I can still fight. However, I am a Christian soldier. I fight for the good of his people. I try to help others see their evil ways and try to help them through it. It is a battle I will never lose because God is with me and the people I am helping. I pray for the Holy Spirit to touch their lives and allow God to do wonderful things for them. When this happens, they repay the favor to someone else. God will do the same for others as He has done for them. That is how God works in the lives of all of us.

You need to treat people the way you want to be treated. There are so many adages handed down through the years that apply to this. Most of them are Bible-based. Particularly the Golden Rule: treat others as you would want to be treated. Watch how you talk to others. Treat people with a kind word. Do a favor for someone without being asked. Control your temper and be aware of the foul language you use.

Before I was a Christian, I had a mouth on me that would make a sailor blush. I swore like there was no tomorrow. I now find myself being offended when someone cusses in front of me especially if they know my beliefs. On the contrary, I appreciate it when someone cusses and then apologizes to me. It shows they respect God and me. It also shows me that they have hope.

I now realize what a fool I made of myself by the language I used. Trust me, you can show more intelligence and gain respect when you use more constructive words. I
go so far as to not watch a movie if they have to use the Lord's name in vain repeatedly. In fact, it amazes me how certain movies have been edited for regular television broadcasts and how they will edit all the cussing except for the Lord's name being used in vain. That there is the devil at work through the networks.

What further bothers me and makes me wonder about some people. It is the fact that there are some people older than me and can't get through a conversation with cussing. They really look ignorant and you have to feel sorry for them. Sorry because they haven't grasped the English language nor have they found Jesus as their savior.

Doing a good deed every day is a lifestyle to live by. Since becoming a Christian I have found that doing the little things for people, come back to you. But you don't necessarily do it for yourself. You do it to give God His glory. By becoming a Christian, you will find yourself acting as Jesus would want you to act. That means treating people nicely. Holding doors open for others, letting someone into your traffic lane, even if they don't have their blinker on. Saying thoughtful things such as "Thank you" and "You're welcome". Calling someone by "sir" or "ma'am".

When you read the Bible, you will discover that it all comes down to just one word. And that is "Love". All you find in it is how to love. Love thy neighbor, love thy mother and father. Love thy spouse. Love can be measured on many different scales. You love your parents, but that is different than how you love your spouse. You love your neighbor but that is different from how you love your children. Love is a wonderful thing. It is at its best when it is given. After all, isn't it better to give than to receive? Again, showing love, just like kindness, will come back to you tenfold.

Since I became a Christian, this part has been very difficult for me. Remember my childhood. I was never shown love, except by my grandmother. So, how can I, who has never received it, learn to give it? It wasn't easy, and it surely didn't happen overnight. But once I asked the Lord to give me this gift of giving love, it has become natural. I find myself doing it without any thought or effort.

First, I had to be willing to accept it. I had to know that I was worthy of love. The first sign that I ever had of being worthy of love, was when I received a hug from the pastor at the church I used to attend in Omaha. At first, I was shocked at the motion. Second, I was unsure, and third, it made me cry when I got home that day. I didn't know how to handle it. But as time went by and the more hugs I received, the better everything felt. I got so comfortable with it that I was looking forward to it. Then I found myself giving them as well.

There is one thing I would like to add that I always got a kick out of. I saw a bumper sticker that read, "Lord, help me become the person my dog thinks I am." If you are a dog owner you might be able to relate to what I am saying. My dog knew that I was her provider and caretaker. She knew that I loved her unconditionally. I gave her what she wanted and needed. I wasn't stubborn. If I got mad at her, she came to me and asked for forgiveness. My relationship with her taught me how to treat others and how to behave. Regardless of my situation or mood, she always loved me unconditionally. It is amazing how God can work through you. He can teach you so many things in so many ways.

God has done so much in my life that I now have a favorite song performed by Mercy Me. That song is titled, "I Can Only Imagine". It tells of what a certain man's reaction would be like once he saw Jesus. Would he stand and sing or will he kneel and pray? It touches my heart each and every time I hear it, no matter how many times. It gives me assurance that I will go to Heaven one day and be able to see Him and speak with Him. The entire event will be the most amazing thing, more than you could ever hope for or dream about.

My life as a Christian has been nothing short of amazing. I thank God for giving me a second chance at life and I try my best every day to make the best of it. I want to do good work for Him and give Him honor and glory. I want to pay Him back for my salvation by helping others and showing them His greatness.

There are many individuals in the Bible who had flaws and yet God found a way to use them all. Jacob was a cheater, David had an affair, Jonah ran from God, Paul was a murderer, Gideon was insecure and Thomas was a doubter.

I would like to close with some scriptures or sayings that have helped me stay strong with my spiritual growth. They may or may not have some reflection on what I have already discussed. However, they were very inspirational to me and I hope they can be for you as well.

Faith is not a feeling, as it is an attitude. It is knowing God. True happiness begins with a relationship with God.

God is a master builder and you are not completed yet and he never quits. Learn to wait on Him. It builds your faith and character.

God is just a prayer away.

God wants to speak to you.

God accepted me as a sinner. What more will he continue to do for me?

Anticipate victory.

He knows we are learning. He knows we will make mistakes. He knows our weaknesses and strengths better than we do.

He is the same yesterday, today, and tomorrow.

He wants a relationship with us more than we do.

God is a King. He is the almighty, all wonderful. He loves us.

Life is full of disappointments. How you handle them is key.

Suffering is purification.

Not having faith in God is displeasing to Him.

Our goal is to get to Heaven, not retire. We should want what God has prepared for us.

His ways are better than our ways.

Can God trust you?

God wants us to need Him.

Our God is an awesome God.

The achievement of your goal is assured, the moment you commit yourself.

You can not go wrong with God. (My favorite)

Good morning, this is God. I will be handling all of your problems today. I will not need your help, so have a wonderful day.

Don't give up too soon, you never know when you're on your way to a miracle.

It doesn't matter what others think of you as much as it matters what God thinks of you.

Weak people revenge, strong people forgive. Intelligent people ignore.

When God says "yes", he builds your faith. When he says "wait", he is building patience. When he says "no", he has something better planned for you

Christianity is the only religion that does not have a man-made God. Remember that.

I want to let you know that God wants a personal relationship with all of us. It is your choice, your free will to make that decision to have this wonderful experience with Him. I pray that you see the light like I have and you go on to do His work. May God Bless You.